THE MIDLAND RAILWAY

Through the Eyes of a Collector

Roy F. Burrows

AMBERLEY

First published 2017

Amberley Publishing
The Hill, Stroud,
Gloucestershire, GL5 4EP

www.amberley-books.com

ISBN: 978 1 4456 5565 9 (print)
ISBN: 978 1 4456 5566 6 (ebook)

British Library Cataloguing in Publication Data.
A catalogue record for this book is available from the British Library.

Typeset in 10pt on 13pt Celeste.
Typesetting by Amberley Publishing.
Printed in the UK.

Contents

Acknowledgements

All the illustrations used in this book are from the Midland Railway Society's records unless otherwise individually acknowledged. I have to thank Dave Harris and Jack Boskett for the photographs they have taken especially for the Society for inclusion in the book. I am also indebted to the following for their help and advice: John Alsop, Tony Furse, David Geldard, Ian Howard, Steve Huson, Tony Overton, Sandra Phipps and David Postle.

Mervyn Bryce, as ever, has been of great help and I have to mention especially the work done by June Cook in so generously using her remarkable skills with digital images, without which a significant number of noteworthy collection items would not have made it onto the pages of the book.

Finally, as always, I am indebted to my wife Anne for her patience with all the keyboard work involved, not only with the script, but in finding, retrieving and sorting the images from the Society's archives.

Bibliography

Burrows, R. F. (Editor), *Midland Railway 150* (Published by the editor, 1994).

Burrows, R. F., *Handbook of Midland Railway Luggage Labels,* 3rd Edition (Railway Print Society (now the Railway Ephemera Society), 2011).

Carter, Oliver, *An Illustrated History of British Railway Hotels 1838–1983* (Silver Link Publishing: Lancashire, 1990).

Froggatt, D. J., *Railway Buttons Badges & Uniforms,* (Ian Allen Ltd: London, 1986) (plus Supplement No. 1, published by the Author 1989).

Geldard, D. G., *Ordinary Single and Return Tickets of the Midland Railway* (Solo Publications: Canterbury, 2008).

Hawthorne, R., *Railway Horse Brasses* (National Horse Brass Society, 1987).

Lyman, I. P., *Railway Clocks* (Mayfield Books: Ashbourne, 2004).

Introduction

The origin of the Midland Railway Collection, on which this book is based, can be traced back to 1945 when, as a twelve-year-old, I began to buy on a regular basis (as they were issued twice a year) the timetables of the Big Four railway companies. Around 1965, I decided to concentrate on acquiring Midland Railway material from the pre-Grouping period (i.e., up to 1923).

Why the Midland? My father started his working life on the Midland Railway at Swadlincote in South Derbyshire after leaving school at fourteen. Although he had left railway service well before I was born, he nevertheless had many stories to tell about his experiences, which, as a very small boy, I found absorbing, asking to hear them over and over again. Thus was my interest in the Midland Railway kindled at a very early age. It grew and matured (some unkind souls would say became an obsession) over a seventy-year period, resulting in a collection of over 43,500 (almost totally Midland) items by January 2016.

In 1994 a cross section of items from the collection was assembled to form an exhibition marking the 150th anniversary of the formation of the Midland Railway. The exhibition (MR 150) opened at the Midland Hotel in Derby, before moving to the Silk Mill – Derby's museum of industry and history – and then on to the National Railway Museum in York. This public exposure led a number of respected members of the railway collecting and preservation movements to note that this was a significant single company collection in the national sense and that it should, if possible, be preserved intact because, if dispersed, it could never be re-formed. Eventually, a way forward was found and in 2000 it became a registered charity, known as the Roy F. Burrows Midland Collection Trust (RFBMCT).

Ten years after MR 150 (in 2004), a co-operative venture was launched by RFBMCT, Derby Museums, and the Midland Railway Society (MRS) to open a Midland Railway Study Centre in the Silk Mill in Derby, based on the RFBMCT collection with additions from the railway collections of both MRS and Derby Museums. During the 1990s the whole collection had been located in my house – a situation that I freely admit would not have been possible had I not been a widower living on my own since 1988! A review in 2014 of future options for the Collection led RFBMCT to propose to MRS (which had by now become a charity in its own right) that the two organisations should merge as a single charity, retaining the title Midland Railway Society. After eighteen months of negotiation

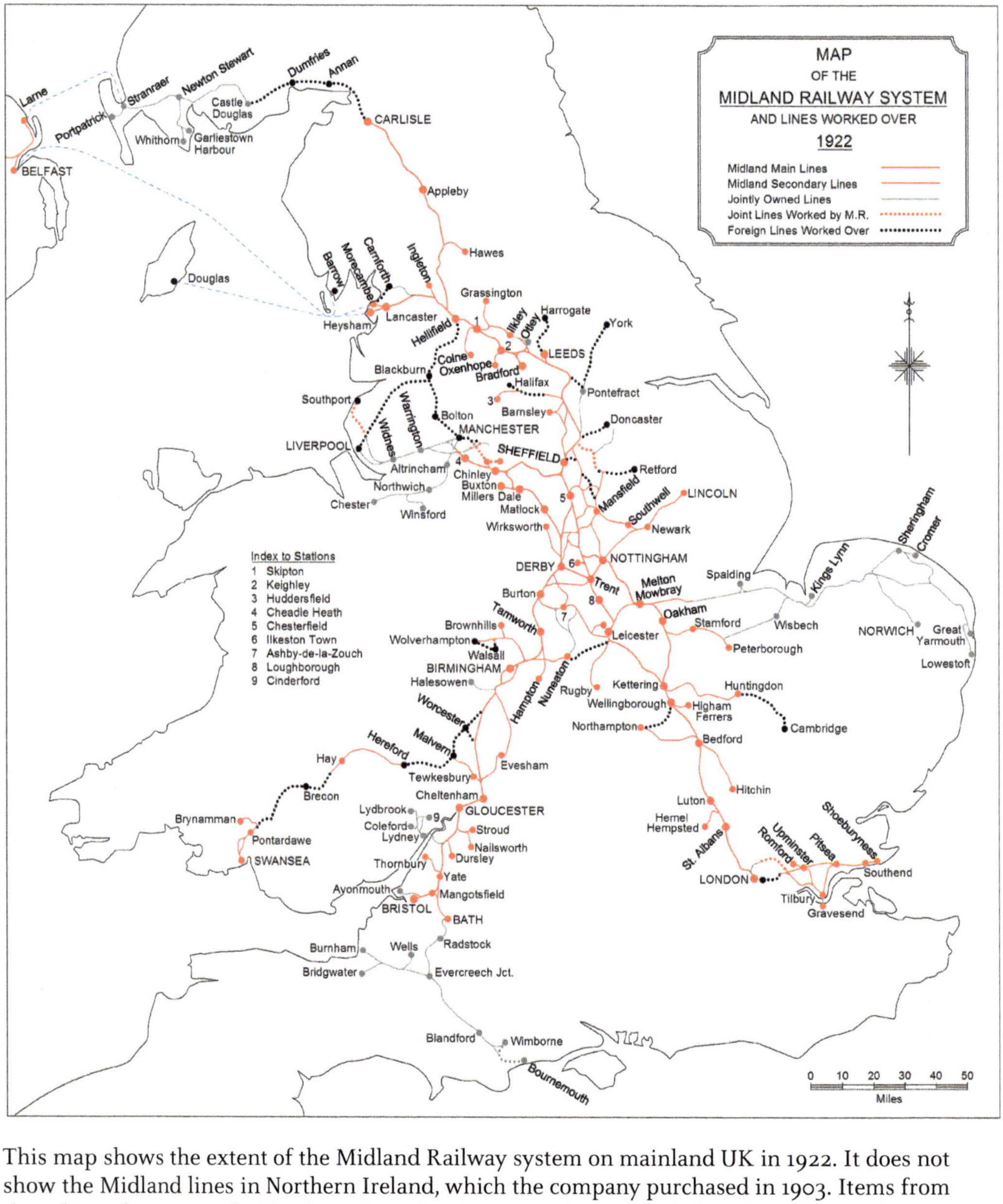

This map shows the extent of the Midland Railway system on mainland UK in 1922. It does not show the Midland lines in Northern Ireland, which the company purchased in 1903. Items from these lines (known as the Northern Counties Committee) are included in the collection but are not featured in this book because of space constraints. (Steve Huson)

and approval by the Charity Commission, the merger was effected on 9 February 2016 and a wholly new Midland Railway Study Centre, managed by the MRS, will be incorporated in the plans for a completely refurbished Silk Mill (to be known as Derby's Museum of Making), for which total grants of £16 million have been obtained from the Heritage Lottery Fund and Arts Council (England).

Clearly, only a relatively small number from a collection of over 53,000 items (now including those Society and Derby Museum items from pre-merger days) can be featured in a book of this size. To try to give a degree of coherence to what is bound to be a somewhat varied selection, I have divided the book into five chapters. For the first two I have selected items to illustrate features of the Midland that would have been visible to the observant traveller making his journey in the years before 1923.

CHAPTER 1 – STATIONS covers the traveller's approach to, and passage through, the station to the platform, including some relevant items from 'behind the scenes'.

CHAPTER 2 – TRAINS covers items to be seen both on his train and through the carriage window.

CHAPTER 3 – PEOPLE deals with items concerned with staff and their welfare.

CHAPTER 4 – HORSES may seem an odd subject for a book such as this. Not so. Even though the development of the steam locomotive running on steel rails was the driving force in the provision of transport facilities in the Victorian age, the importance of the horse did not disappear with the demise of the stagecoach. The 'first mile' and the 'last mile' in the conveyance of goods from manufacturer to customer were entirely dependent on the horse. While the end of the First World War saw the beginnings of the use of motor transport for the delivery and collection of goods and parcels to and from stations, it was not until after the end of the Second World War in the late 1940s that horse-drawn vehicles finally disappeared from use.

CHAPTER 5 – HOTELS AND CATERING deals with an important adjunct to the main business of the pre-Grouping railway, which was the provision of hotel accommodation and catering facilities for the traveller. A whole range of 'domestic' equipment was required for these services and a selection of appropriate items is featured in this chapter.

Hopefully, today's reader will thus get a feel for the extensive range and variety of activities necessary to sustain the country's primary transport system of over 100 years ago. I have deliberately minimised coverage of the more technical aspects of the steam railway, such as locomotives, carriages and signalling, because much has already been published on these subjects – although it has to be said that a definitive work on Midland signalling practice has yet to be written.

For those readers who, after reading this book, would like to learn more about the full extent of the collection, there is a complete catalogue of all the items located on the Study Centre website www.midlandrailwaystudycentre.org.uk. For readers who would like to know more about the Society itself, please visit www.midlandrailwaysociety.org.uk.

CHAPTER 1

Stations

Stations in their various forms were the public face of the railway and, in the larger towns and cities, were often the dominant architectural feature of their neighbourhood. No two stations were the same, although, during the time J. H. Sanders was in post as the company architect, from 1852 until his death in 1884, many stations were built with common features. Even today this is particularly noticeable with the stations on the Settle & Carlisle line built in the 1870s.

Most stations dealt with both passenger and goods traffic, and separate buildings were provided for each. However, in the cities, entirely separate goods stations were provided.

As a reference point, linking stations to objects in the collection, I have selected St Pancras as an example of the large multi-platform urban passenger station. By way of contrast, at the other end of the scale, is the small country station at Cleeve, on the main line between Ashchurch and Cheltenham, which did cater for both passenger and goods traffic, but was some 2 miles from the village of Bishop's Cleeve from which it took its name.

Our traveller's introduction to the Midland may well have been by means of one or more posters, which were used as a major means of advertising, particularly on boards or hoardings on railway property visible to the public. Stations were, of course, prime sites in this context and station approaches and platforms were used to full effect. Tens of thousands of posters were printed over the years, covering a vast range of subjects, including holiday resorts, train excursions, cheap tickets, alterations to train services and many more. A small selection of Midland posters from the collection is illustrated (see pp. 9–10).

Our intending passenger would probably have selected the train on which to travel by reference to the Midland's public timetables, which were on sale at stations and town offices. Many different versions were produced over the years and a selection is illustrated (see pp. 11–12).

Entry to the station would have been via the booking hall, within which the booking office window – or windows, as in the case of a large station such as St Pancras – were located (see p. 13). The positions of the actual windows are indicated by the small 'crush barriers'; in this view the windows themselves have their decorative shutters in place. A rather simpler window was used at smaller stations. An example from the Midland's station at Cheltenham (Lansdown) is shown on p. 13, both after its removal intact from the original lath and plaster wall, and in its current position at the Study Centre.

A selection of Midland posters from the collection.

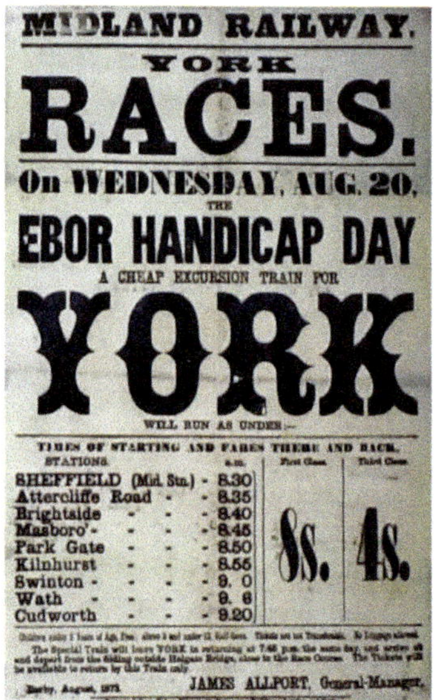

A selection of Midland posters from the collection.

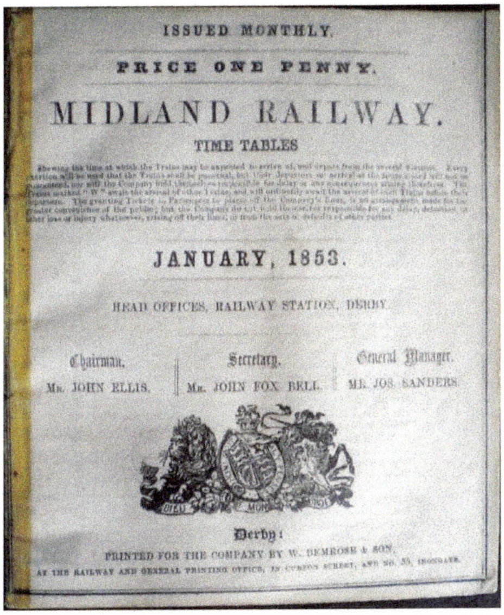

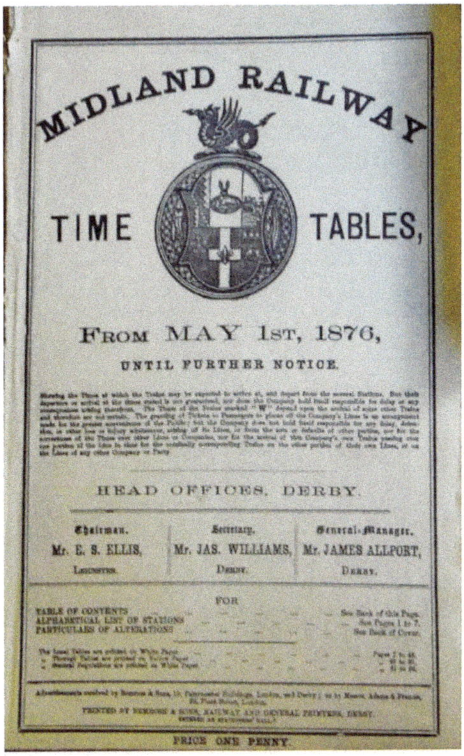

The four principal styles of Midland public timetables through the life of the company.

A selection of the various types of regional / local timetables published over the years.

St Pancras booking office.

Booking office window at the former Cheltenham Lansdown station (left) and as subsequently restored (right).

Also in the booking hall and/or waiting room would have been one or more display boards containing sheet timetables of the train services on lines serving the station. An example of a Midland glass-framed display board for use indoors containing a later (1929) LMS timetable of the former Midland Main Line is also shown below. Pictured, too, is a fully restored, more robust non-glass fronted board used at outside locations exposed to the weather.

Changes were made to the booking hall at St Pancras by British Rail in the 1980s and, in the process, a pair of original doors became redundant. These are believed to be the ones in the far wall in the image on p. 16. They contained a set of brass door furniture of 1868 vintage with the 'court jester' design of decoration. Fortunately, these were saved from the scrapyard by the contractor and are now in the Study Centre. Replicas were produced for use at the new St Pancras and can be seen on doors along the walkway beside Sir John Betjeman's statue.

Time is of the essence in the railway business and, in Midland days, large clocks were very evident on station platforms – particularly at the bigger stations. Wall clocks were also necessary in most offices and certainly in every signal box. Unfortunately, the Midland was the only major pre-Grouping railway company not to number each of its clocks, and thus a clock register was not maintained. It is therefore only possible to guess at the number it owned – the late Ian Lyman, in his standard work on *Railway Clocks* (see bibliography), could do no better than guess at 'several thousand'. Pictured opposite are three examples of Midland clocks in the collection. The vast majority of clocks bought by the Midland were obtained from John Smith & Sons of Derby, particularly in later years. Unlike those of other railways, they were not usually marked with the company's initials on either the dial or case, although a few exceptions have survived.

Our prospective passenger, having confirmed his train times by reference to the sheet timetable, would then have bought a ticket for his journey at the booking office window. It is

Midland Railway display boards.

Above left: A 12-inch-dial dropcase clock by Thomas Rock of Derby, acquired by the late George Dow from the original station at Rowsley and believed to date from 1849. George fixed a brass plate on the front to record the provenance of the clock.

Below left: This much later 12-inch-dial dropcase clock is unusually marked with the company's name in full on the dial.

Right: An early (*c.* 1875) long case clock by Reuben Bosworth of Nottingham. This was clearly an 'item of furniture' intended to grace the office of a senior manager and was last in railway service in the Goods Manager's office in Nottingham. Similar weight-driven clocks were also supplied by Bosworth and used in Midland signal boxes but they were frugal examples in painted pine cases with no decorative features. (Talisman Railwayana Auctions)

Above: St Pancras booking hall.

Left: Original brass door furniture from St Pancras booking hall, mounted to show the 'court jester' pattern engraving. Finger plate on the right.

An interior view of the reconstructed Alvechurch booking office at Kidderminster Railway Museum.

Examples of items of office equipment on display in the Alvechurch booking office. All are marked with the company's name or initials, including the inkwells, pen and pencils. The wall-mounted telephone has an angled message pad tray at the base. The lower right illustration is of a ticket dating machine, used to print the date of issue on Edmondson tickets. A box of type was provided for the booking clerk to manually change the numbers and letters in the machine at the start of each day and month respectively. Also shown is a pair of manual ticket nippers.

appropriate to look behind the window at the interior of a typical Midland booking office. Fortunately, Kidderminster Railway Museum (KRM) have recreated a Midland booking office using original fixtures recovered from Alvechurch. The Society has provided, on loan from the collection, a large number of the artefacts used to create the interior display as it would have appeared in Midland Railway days. A general view is shown on p. 17, while some of the various items of office equipment and other fixtures on view are shown individually.

Every station was issued with a fares book, which listed all the stations to which tickets could be issued, with the applicable single and return fares for each recognised route where there was a choice. The book for St Pancras with a pair of open pages is illustrated. The standard form of ticket was the serially numbered $2\frac{1}{4}$ x $1\frac{3}{16}$ inch card invented by Thomas Edmondson in 1839, of which many millions were produced at the company's ticket printing office in Derby.

From 1902 onwards, the standard colour for first class single tickets was yellow and that for third class single tickets was khaki, officially known as 'drab'. Some examples of fully pre-printed tickets to and from stations mentioned in this chapter are shown (see opposite). In addition, 'blank card' tickets were provided for use where journeys were infrequent. These were pre-printed with the name of the issuing station, leaving the destination, route and fare to be completed by the booking clerk by reference to the station fares book.

Tickets awaiting issue were stored in special cupboards or racks at the side of the ticket window (see illustration on p. 17 where the rack is on the right of the window with the tambour-type sliding door closed). This example is one of the smallest Midland ticket racks. Racks at the larger stations could be of considerable size but, because each had to be easily accessible to the booking clerk, there was an effective limit to the number

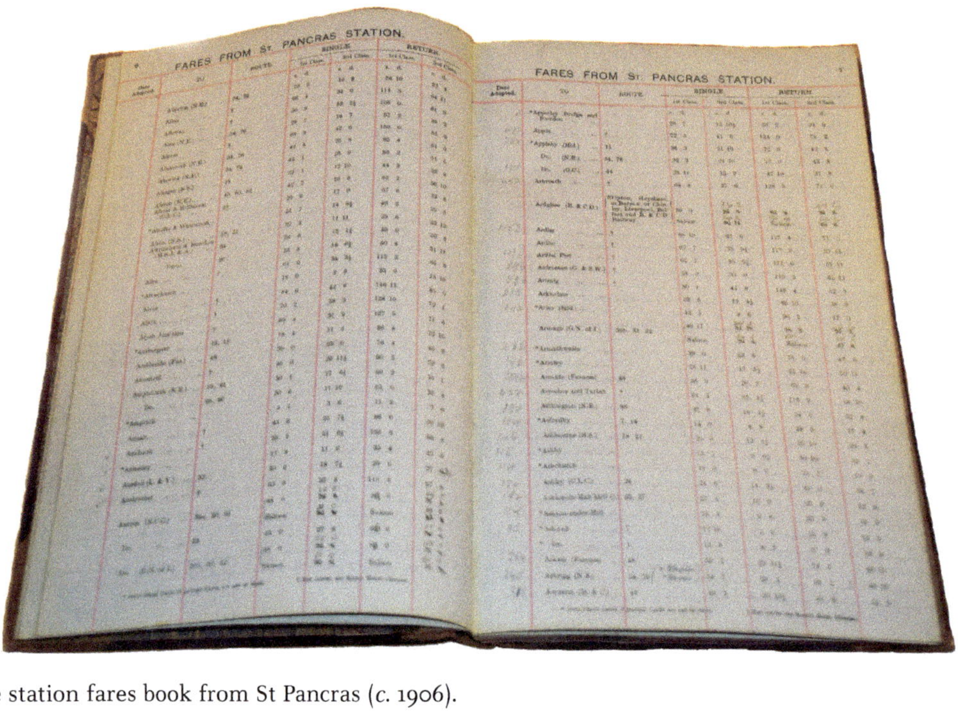

The station fares book from St Pancras (*c.* 1906).

Six examples of Midland Edmondson tickets. Ticket 1190 is for one of the shortest journeys on the Midland, between Derby and Derby (Nottingham Road) – a distance of 58 chains (just under ¾ mile). By comparison, ticket 027 is for a journey of 574 miles. Ticket 1655 is an unusual choice for a journey from London to Cheltenham but the fare of 9s 6*d* was the same as that from Paddington by the GWR. The fact that pre-printed tickets were provided indicates more than just a few persons chose the Midland route from London to Cheltenham via Birmingham.

and size of racks per window. Where the volume of passengers was high, more than one window would be provided (each with its own racks), as at St Pancras.

David Geldard, the recognised authority on UK pre-Grouping railway tickets, has provided the Society with a complete catalogue of known Midland Railway tickets with every type described and illustrated in full colour. This has been deposited in the Study Centre and is regularly updated. It is available for research and study by appointment. In addition, David has published a reference book on *Ordinary Single and Return Tickets of the Midland Railway* (see bibliography).

On leaving the booking office at a large station, having obtained his ticket, the passenger would be met by an array of signs indicating the whereabouts of amenities and various offices, as well as many advertising posters and enamels. Offices would have identifying door plates fitted. Hanging signs were usually double-sided, as were those fixed to brackets

A selection of Midland enamel door plates and signs. Note the characteristic white border on the door plates. The mountings for the two lower double-sided enamels are modern.

projecting from the wall. Some representative examples of Midland door plates and other signs from the collection are shown.

A large number of Victorian passengers did not 'travel light' and trunks and large suitcases were the norm, particularly if a family was travelling together. There was not

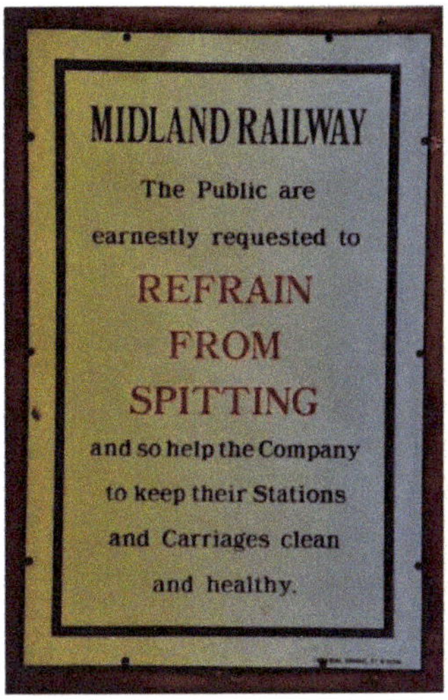

A selection of signs, which were fixed to walls. The top three (the top left is enamel, the other two cast iron) are a reminder of the prevalence of tuberculosis among the population in the Victorian era. The lower sign is from the halfway bifurcation point on the staircase from the footbridge to the Up platform at Bingley.

room in the carriages of that time for such large (and heavy) luggage – the luggage van or guard's van was provided for the purpose. Each piece of luggage had to be clearly labelled so that it 'followed the passenger' – particularly important when changes of train were necessary. To help in the management of luggage in this way, luggage labels (pre-printed with the destination station) were stocked in special racks at stations. The racks at St Pancras were sited in the booking hall and can be seen on the far wall in the illustration on p. 16. The labels were selected and stuck onto luggage as appropriate by the porter, who would then place it on the train – a precise parallel, in fact, with the modern airline baggage tag. Examples of Midland luggage labels are shown below. A full description of the various types of Midland luggage labels is given in the *Handbook of Midland Railway Luggage Labels* (see bibliography).

A weight- and size-limited service for parcels by passenger train was provided at a higher price than the one charged for transit by the slower goods trains. The parcels office was the point on the station where this traffic was co-ordinated. At the larger stations it had its own

A selection of Midland luggage labels.

external entrance, and provided local collection and delivery services by horse-drawn carts. Parcels were also accepted 'over the counter' from members of the public and the scale of charges was displayed. Every parcel had to be weighed, and examples of the smaller type of scales used by the Midland for this purpose are shown overleaf.

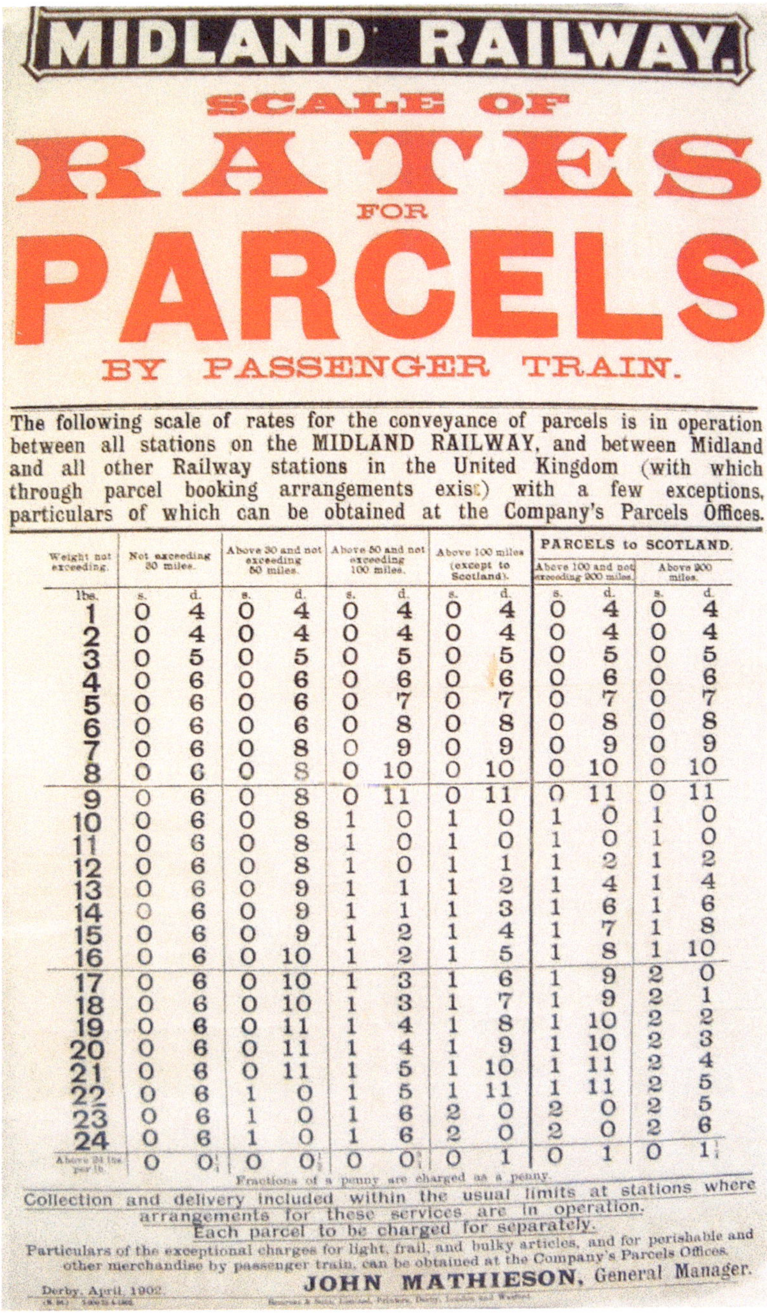

MIDLAND RAILWAY.

SCALE OF RATES FOR PARCELS BY PASSENGER TRAIN.

The following scale of rates for the conveyance of parcels is in operation between all stations on the MIDLAND RAILWAY, and between Midland and all other Railway stations in the United Kingdom (with which through parcel booking arrangements exist) with a few exceptions, particulars of which can be obtained at the Company's Parcels Offices.

Weight not exceeding.	Not exceeding 30 miles.		Above 30 and not exceeding 50 miles.		Above 50 and not exceeding 100 miles.		Above 100 miles (except to Scotland).		PARCELS to SCOTLAND. Above 100 and not exceeding 200 miles.		PARCELS to SCOTLAND. Above 200 miles.	
lbs.	s.	d.	s.	d.	s.	d.	s.	d.	s.	d.	s.	d.
1	0	4	0	4	0	4	0	4	0	4	0	4
2	0	4	0	4	0	4	0	4	0	4	0	4
3	0	5	0	5	0	5	0	5	0	5	0	5
4	0	6	0	6	0	6	0	6	0	6	0	6
5	0	6	0	6	0	7	0	7	0	7	0	7
6	0	6	0	6	0	8	0	8	0	8	0	8
7	0	6	0	8	0	9	0	9	0	9	0	9
8	0	6	0	8	0	10	0	10	0	10	0	10
9	0	6	0	8	0	11	0	11	0	11	0	11
10	0	6	0	8	1	0	1	0	1	0	1	0
11	0	6	0	8	1	0	1	0	1	0	1	0
12	0	6	0	8	1	0	1	1	1	2	1	2
13	0	6	0	9	1	1	1	2	1	4	1	4
14	0	6	0	9	1	1	1	3	1	6	1	6
15	0	6	0	9	1	2	1	4	1	7	1	8
16	0	6	0	10	1	2	1	5	1	8	1	10
17	0	6	0	10	1	3	1	6	1	9	2	0
18	0	6	0	10	1	3	1	7	1	9	2	1
19	0	6	0	11	1	4	1	8	1	10	2	2
20	0	6	0	11	1	4	1	9	1	10	2	3
21	0	6	0	11	1	5	1	10	1	11	2	4
22	0	6	1	0	1	5	1	11	1	11	2	5
23	0	6	1	0	1	6	2	0	2	0	2	5
24	0	6	1	0	1	6	2	0	2	0	2	6
Above 24 lbs. per lb.	0	0¼	0	0½	0	0¾	0	1	0	1	0	1¼

Fractions of a penny are charged as a penny.

Collection and delivery included within the usual limits at stations where arrangements for these services are in operation.

Each parcel to be charged for separately.

Particulars of the exceptional charges for light, frail, and bulky articles, and for perishable and other merchandise by passenger train, can be obtained at the Company's Parcels Offices.

Derby, April, 1902.

JOHN MATHIESON, General Manager.

A poster displaying the charges for sending parcels by passenger train.

The parcels office and cloak room sign is a wooden hanging sign with cast letters. The colours are those of the BR (LMR) era. The lower views are of various scales, all marked with the company's name or initials. Although the dial of the lower scale is marked 'LMS', the integrally cast letters 'M' and 'R' on either side reveal its origin.

Milk was a perishable commodity. Rapid transport of large quantities was now possible by rail from country areas to large towns and cities. The availability of fresh milk on a daily basis helped bring about a significant improvement in the general health of the population in industrial urban areas. Milk was conveyed in large churns (cylindrical or conical metal containers). They were brought from local farms by horse and cart to country stations, and loaded in special milk vans to be conveyed to city goods stations. The image below shows this activity taking place at Idridgehay, a country station on the Wirksworth branch in Derbyshire. The image overleaf shows churns at the other end of their journey being handled at Somerstown goods station, next to St Pancras in London. The Society has two churns in the collection, and the images demonstrate how the lid was secured and labelled with brass fittings showing the name of the dairy in London (F. & C. Dairy Co., St Pancras) and the station for return to the owner when empty; in this case J. Hutchinson at Chellaston, a station south of Derby on the Melbourne branch.

The building at the wayside station at Cleeve (see p. 27) is the original, dating from the opening of the station in 1843. Clearly it provided minimal accommodation, probably only consisting of a stationmaster's office and waiting room. The entrance door was at the south end of the building and the single chimney stack indicates a fireplace was provided. An early type of cast-iron Victorian fireplace used by the Midland at country stations has been fully restored, together with a metal fender (see p. 28). Something similar may have been installed at Cleeve. Photographic evidence clearly establishes that this building remained unaltered for over 100 years until closure in 1950.

Loading milk churns at Idridgehay – a photograph that shows the extent of milk traffic at a country station in the Victorian era.

Above: Handling milk churns at Somerstown.

Left: The lid of a milk churn.

Cleeve station in 1884. (Bernard Mathews Collection, courtesy Ian Howard)

Cleeve station in 1937. (Ian Howard)

A Midland cast-iron fireplace.

A Midland cast-iron fireplace fender.

Midland enamel Gentlemen sign in wooden frame.

All the station services described earlier would have been provided (on an appropriately reduced scale) from this one building, probably by the stationmaster himself, for whom the company provided a house close by (behind the bridge abutment on the left). A later photograph, taken in 1937 (see p. 27), again looking south but from the other side of the bridge, shows more clearly the platforms, signal box and, in the distance, the goods yard. Cleeve platforms are devoid of signage with one exception: a rather forlorn projecting sign, 'GENTLEMEN', signifying the availability of a circular urinal, constructed of cast iron and open to the elements: basic indeed! A similar sign (but with enamel lettering) from the collection is shown above. No surviving plans of Cleeve station have yet been seen, so whether any ladies' facilities were ever provided in the small station building is a moot point.

Cleeve was one of the Midland country stations that retained oil lamps as a means of illumination throughout its existence. The Midland platform lamp standards and their lanterns are clearly shown in the photographs. Oil lamps would be lit at dusk and placed inside the platform lanterns, to be extinguished after the last train had departed in the evening. In some locations it was more convenient to use wall-mounted lanterns on platforms, as demonstrated in the illustration on p. 30. The one with the filigree decoration around the top represents a design so far noted as only having been used at Matlock Bath. Sometimes the front glass face of the lantern would have the top section etched with the name of the station in blue. Close study of the original photograph shows this may have been the case at Cleeve.

Internal illumination in offices and waiting rooms was also achieved by means of oil lamps. Two types are illustrated. One is wall-mounted using a cast iron bracket (see p. 30) and the other is, in effect, a desktop or table lamp (see p. 32). Both used identical brass reservoirs and burners.

It is appropriate to mention the ubiquitous paraffin hand lamp, of which there were two basic types: the general purpose lamp (see p. 31) designed to give general illumination and the directional three-aspect lamp. Most staff on outside duty at night would carry a hand lamp. The 'small' pattern, unrestored, three-aspect lamp (also shown on p. 31) was personalised for use by Inspector Marshall, Gloucester. Red or green (as well as clear) lights could be displayed by rotating the handle relative to the circular body. This action moved the appropriately coloured curved glass in front of the flame.

Two different patterns of Midland wall-mounted external oil lamp casings.

Above: A brass oil lamp reservoir and burner from Evesham (Midland Railway) station, probably used in an outside lantern.

Left: MR interior wall-mounted oil lamp.

MR general purpose hand lamp.

MR three-aspect hand lamp.

MR table oil lamp.

Chapter 2

Trains

No. 1004 standing in the centre road at Leicester in 1909, waiting to take over the 9.30 a.m. Scotch express from St Pancras. This was the last of the original batch of five of the ubiquitous 4-4-0 'Midland compounds', as designed by S. W. Johnson. Subsequently over 1,200 were built by both the Midland and LMS companies. The arrow indicates the position of the builder's plate – see p. 35. (Ian Howard)

Having arrived on the appropriate platform, our observant passenger would have noticed several features of the Midland locomotive as it drew his train to a halt. To set these features in context I have selected a photograph of locomotive No. 1004, principally because the number plate fixed on the smokebox door has survived and is now in the collection. This type of plate was a unique feature of Midland locomotives in pre-Grouping days. After 1923, the LMS adopted the feature throughout the company and still later, after nationalisation in 1948, smokebox number plates were applied to the entire fleet of British Railways steam locomotives. The LMS continued the Midland-style serif numbers, but BR chose a sans serif style.

The Midland allocated a number to each of their main locomotive sheds; the home depot of each locomotive was identified by a small, oval, cast-iron 'shed code' plate fixed to the lower part of the smokebox door. It so happens that No. 1004 was a Leeds engine at the time of the photograph and so the actual plate would have been a number 28. Smaller sheds were sometimes allocated suffix letters to the main shed number, although this scheme was not fully developed until LMS days and, like smokebox number plates, it was also introduced across all regions after nationalisation.

Arranged on the front of the locomotive would be one or more oil-burning headlamps to identify the class of train. For passenger trains there were two configurations: two lamps

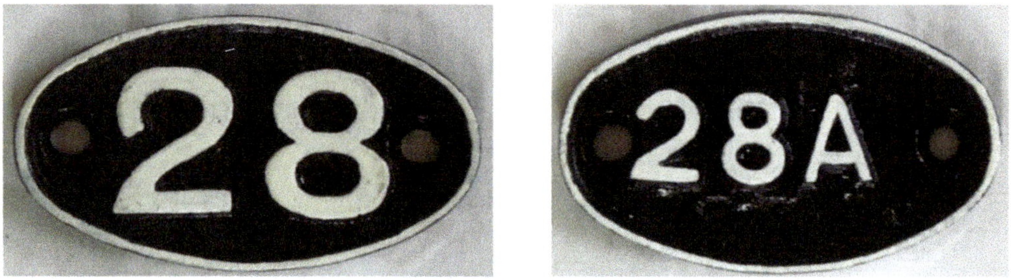

Two Midland 'shed code' plates (28 – Leeds; 28A – Stourton).

Three Midland smokebox number plates.

An LMS locomotive headlamp, identical to the Midland design.

(one over each buffer) for express trains and a single lamp at the top of the smokebox for slow (stopping) trains. Other configurations applied to goods trains. The Midland design of locomotive headlamp was perpetuated without change right up until the end of steam in British Rail days.

All locomotives were fitted with builders' plates. Each railway company had their own design, which recorded the company name (or initials) and the year of manufacture. The Midland's basic design was oval and cast in brass, although detail variations did occur over the years. In the main, they were located on each side of the boiler mounting at the foot of the smokebox; however, with some classes, they were mounted on the splashers.

Each of the carriages forming the train also carried builders' plates, but they were fixed somewhat out of view of our passenger on the solebar below door level. The same design was used on goods wagons. Also fixed to the end of the carriage was a cast-iron plate, giving its dimensions and, in some cases, the weight (see overleaf).

Two examples of Midland locomotive builders' plates.

Four examples of the standard design of Midland builders' plates used on both passenger and goods vehicles.

A Midland carriage dimension plate.

A Midland carriage weight and dimension plate.

Prominent inside the carriage compartment would be the overhead luggage rack, consisting of netting supported by wooden poles fixed to cast-brass (or iron) brackets, which incorporated the wyvern. The image below shows a version of such a rack constructed for display at MR 150; it uses original Midland brackets with netting from later BR days but is still representative of the nineteenth-century design. It is now in the Study Centre.

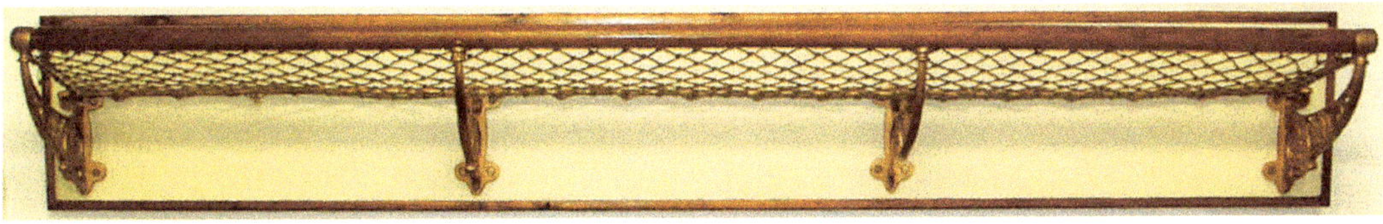

A reconstructed Midland carriage compartment luggage rack.

On the compartment wall, above the seat but below the luggage rack, were mounted carriage prints. These were attractive views of places served by the railway. The Midland used photographs, either sepia or coloured by Photochrom. Sometimes the spaces were used to advertise the hotels and other services provided by the company.

When compartments were heated by steam piped from the locomotive, the amount of heat was controlled by the passenger operating a brass handle on the compartment wall (see p. 38). Access to the compartments of a corridor coach was by an internal sliding door fitted with a decorative brass plate and handle (see p. 39).

Lavatory compartments were provided at the ends of the corridor and a typical frosted glass window incorporating the wyvern in the design is shown on p. 40.

A single-panel Midland carriage print of Peterborough Cathedral by Photochrom.

A two-panel Midland carriage print with views of Ashford and Monsal Dale.

A two-panel Midland carriage print with two views of Cheltenham.

A Midland carriage compartment steam-heating control.

A decorative brass sliding door handle used on a Midland interior compartment door (on a modern display mounting).

A small gas cooker from the attendant's compartment of a Midland sleeping carriage.

A Midland compartment coach lavatory window mounted in a modern frame.

When passengers were travelling long distances overnight in ordinary carriages, they could hire from the larger stations both pillows and rugs. Some of the latter have survived. The official instructions relating to the administration of this relatively minor service are printed here, which neatly illustrate a point made later in Chapter 3 about the extent of paperwork systems used by railways in every aspect of their business.

An example of a rug available for hire by travellers on overnight trains. One of five different examples in the collection.

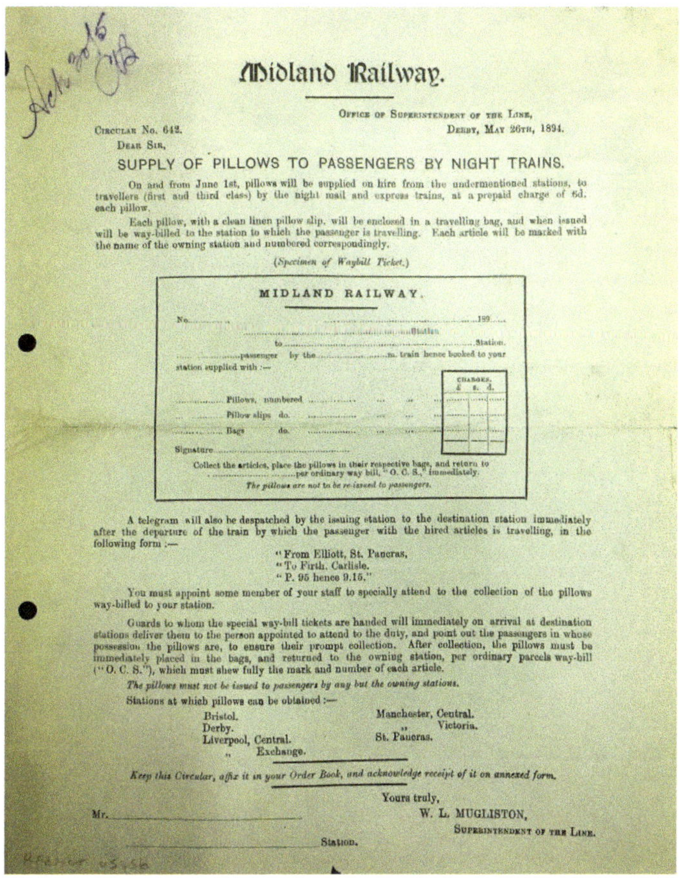

Midland Railway.

Office of Superintendent of the Line,
Derby, May 26th, 1894.

Circular No. 642.

Dear Sir,

SUPPLY OF PILLOWS TO PASSENGERS BY NIGHT TRAINS.

On and from June 1st, pillows will be supplied on hire from the undermentioned stations, to travellers (first and third class) by the night mail and express trains, at a prepaid charge of 6d. each pillow.

Each pillow, with a clean linen pillow slip, will be enclosed in a travelling bag, and when issued will be way-billed to the station to which the passenger is travelling. Each article will be marked with the name of the owning station and numbered correspondingly.

(*Specimen of Waybill Ticket.*)

MIDLAND RAILWAY.

No.............. ....189.....

....Station

to..Station.

..............passenger by the..............m. train hence booked to your station supplied with :—

	Charges £	s.	d.
..............Pillows, numbered			
..............Pillow slips do.			
..............Bags do.			

Signature..

Collect the articles, place the pillows in their respective bags, and return to ....per ordinary way bill, "O. C. S.," immediately.

The pillows are not to be re-issued to passengers.

A telegram will also be despatched by the issuing station to the destination station immediately after the departure of the train by which the passenger with the hired articles is travelling, in the following form :—

"From Elliott, St. Pancras,
"To Firth, Carlisle.
"P. 95 hence 9.15."

You must appoint some member of your staff to specially attend to the collection of the pillows way-billed to your station.

Guards to whom the special way-bill tickets are handed will immediately on arrival at destination stations deliver them to the person appointed to attend to the duty, and point out the passengers in whose possession the pillows are, to ensure their prompt collection. After collection, the pillows must be immediately placed in the bags, and returned to the owning station, per ordinary parcels way-bill ("O. C. S."), which must shew fully the mark and number of each article.

The pillows must not be issued to passengers by any but the owning stations.

Stations at which pillows can be obtained :—

Bristol.
Derby.
Liverpool, Central.
" Exchange.
Manchester, Central.
" Victoria.
St. Pancras.

Keep this Circular, affix it in your Order Book, and acknowledge receipt of it on annexed form.

Yours truly,
W. L. MUGLISTON,
Superintendent of the Line.

Mr...

....Station.

Official instructions detailing the procedure for the hire of pillows to passengers on overnight trains.

Sleeping carriages were provided on the Midland's Anglo-Scottish services. Each had a small compartment for an attendant that was equipped with a small gas cooker. This enabled early morning tea to be provided for sleeping berth passengers. One such fully restored item is in the collection (see p. 39).

Having selected a window seat in his chosen compartment, our traveller would have been able to relax and see the many objects by the lineside that exhibited characteristic Midland features. By statute all railways had to be marked by mileposts at quarter-mile intervals. The Midland's final designs (introduced in the early 1900s) were distinctive and larger (and hence more visible) than those of most other companies. They were mounted on the top of old rails set vertically in the ground by the side of the track. Where clearances were restricted (e.g., on bridges or in tunnels), a flat-plate version was provided. A set of rules were laid down so that all distances were normally measured from zero at St Pancras by the shortest route, although the complex nature of the network made it necessary to establish a few other 'zero' points. The most famous is the zero milepost at London Road Junction, Derby (still *in situ* in 2016 at the south end of the station).

Above Left: This photograph is of a 'whole' milepost *in situ*, mounted on top of an old rail. The location is the end of the truncated branch from Sheepbridge, north of Chesterfield, to Monkwood Colliery and shows the location as 150 miles from zero at St Pancras. The rigid application of the rules often led to minor branch lines such as this being, somewhat incongruously, 'miled' from St Pancras. (Ian Howard)

Above Right: Examples of 'standard' Midland milepost tops. The versions with the circular pediment indicated that the mileage was measured from a 'zero' other than St Pancras (or Derby, in the case of the 'west branch', as the line from there to Bristol was known in Midland days).

Right: Examples of 'flat plate' mileposts used in locations with limited clearance.

Below Left: Examples of Midland bridge plates.

Below Right: Examples of Midland culvert plates (smaller than bridge plates and distinguished by rounded corners).The origin of the anomalous 85 plate (no suffix) is not known.

Every bridge and tunnel on a particular line was numbered sequentially and marked by a cast-iron 'bridge plate'. By contrast with mileposts, these were simple square or rectangular plates. Where a new bridge was erected after the line was constructed (e.g., a station footbridge), it would be identified by a letter suffix to the immediately preceding bridge number. Every drainage culvert under the track was similarly numbered by a smaller cast-iron plate, bearing the preceding bridge number followed by a letter suffix.

Every tunnel was identified by name and its sequential line 'bridge' number. A nameplate (also giving the length of the tunnel) was mounted on, or close to, each portal. The early design was a very heavy solid casting, incorporating the name, length and number of the tunnel. It was later succeeded by a plate using riveted cast letters and numbers to record just the name and length.

A common cast-iron sign was the 'Trespass Notice' to be found at every road and footpath crossing, and other locations where the public might inadvertently stray onto the railway, including the ends of most station platforms. They were often accompanied on the same post with a 'Beware of Trains' sign. Several variants of Midland trespass signs have survived and examples are shown here. All railways were large landowners and often, due to the vagaries of the parliamentary procedures for acquiring land in the first place, the boundaries were not simply marked by normal fencing. In such cases special boundary markers (usually of cast iron) were used and set firmly into the ground (see p. 46).

A common trackside sign was the gradient post (also p. 46). Its purpose was to indicate a change of level of the track to remind the engine driver of the need to increase power

An example of the early design of Midland tunnel plate (unrestored).

The later standard design of Midland tunnel plate.

(or reduce by applying the brakes in the case of a descent). This information was particularly relevant in the days of loose-coupled goods trains (i.e., they were not fitted with continuous brakes), where considerable skill was required by the driver to prevent either stalling on rising grades or excessive speed on descents.

It is beyond the scope of this book to describe Midland signalling practice, but their signals were distinctive and a major feature of the lineside that was often very noticeable from the train. Three illustrations are, therefore, included. One is of a fully working Midland signal from the collection, currently on loan to the St Albans Signal Box Museum (see p. 47). This

Examples of Midland trespass signs.

Examples of Midland boundary markers.

A Midland gradient post.

A fully working restored Midland signal. (St Albans Signal Box Trust)

Left: This photograph is of two Midland signals in actual use at Upton-upon-Severn. The unusual arrangement of the arms on the pole allows both the front and rear arrangements to be clearly visible on the one image.

Below: A gantry of Midland signals at Derby South Junction.

Midland Railway telegraph insulators. The left-hand insulator is of the same pattern as those used on the post illustrated. The other two bear the dates 1880 and 1888 respectively.

should be compared with the view of signals at an actual trackside location (see p. 48). By way of contrast, a splendid array of signals on an original Midland wooden gantry at Derby South Junction is also included.

An object that could be viewed in its hundreds from the train in the early years of the twentieth century, but which has now virtually disappeared from the landscape, is the humble telegraph / telephone insulator – once an essential fixture on every telegraph pole throughout the country (not just on the railways). Several examples used over the years by the Midland are illustrated (see p. 49), together with a superb array of insulators that formed the terminations of the various telegraph circuits of the Midland Railway outside the central telegraph office at Derby on Platform 1 (just out of the picture).

Finally, our passenger, during his journey, could not have missed seeing many goods trains on adjacent tracks and in marshalling yards. The traffic carried by these trains was more significant to the company, in terms of income and profit, than the carriage of passengers. The Midland served many industrial areas that owed their existence to the presence of coal, and their prosperity to the railways, which provided the means for both raw materials and finished products to reach ever-expanding markets.

The coalfields of Nottinghamshire and Derbyshire in particular generated large volumes of traffic for the Midland Railway, especially for destinations in Greater London. The length and frequency of loaded coal trains between Toton marshalling yards near Nottingham and Cricklewood in North London (together with returning empties) are now legendary. The view included below shows loaded coal wagons in one group of Toton sidings and gives a powerful visual impression of the magnitude of the Midland's coal traffic.

Coal traffic at Toton in Midland Railway days.

A selection of wagon labels relating to coal traffic from over 600 of all types in the collection. The lower reversible label is a much larger non-standard label.

Space precludes more than just a token reference to collection items concerned with the vitally important goods traffic. I have chosen to select examples of wagon labels as a way to illustrate the diversity of origins and destinations, and also the wide nature of the traffic conveyed by the ubiquitous goods train.

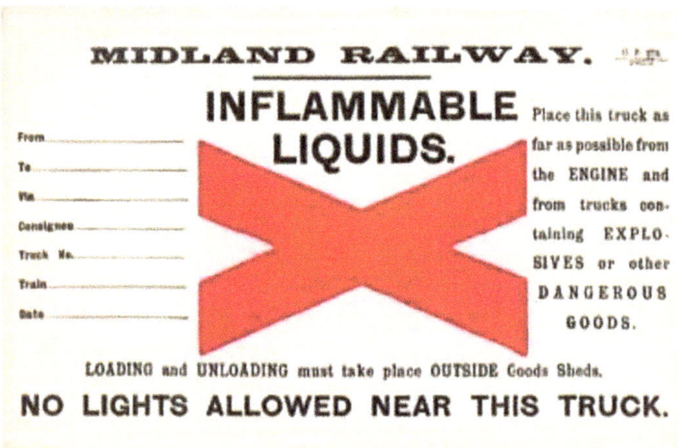

A selection of wagon labels relating to goods traffic of a non-mineral nature. The lower large label is an example used for dangerous traffic. There was a similar label for explosives (with a red circle instead of an 'X').

A selection of tinplate wagon labels, which were permanently fixed to wagons to obviate re-labelling for every empty return trip to the colliery.

Chapter 3

People

The railways were very large employers of labour and, in 1921, the Midland had a total of 84,496 employees (including Northern Ireland). Uniforms identified both the job and seniority of employees, particularly those who came into contact with the public, who were the front-line 'face' of the company at stations, on board trains and in the company's hotels.

There were, of course, very many thousands of staff without uniform who were involved in the design, making and maintaining of locomotives, rolling stock, signalling, buildings, track and other infrastructure. However, among this group – particularly those who worked outside, visible informal indication of seniority as foremen, inspectors and senior managers was evident by the wearing of bowler hats (and, where appropriate, long raincoats!).

A large and vital group of non-uniformed employees were the clerks who were to be found in all departments of the company. The ability to communicate effectively between large numbers of people in a complex organisation, spread over a wide geographical area, was fundamental to the success of a railway company such as the Midland. The written word was the only effective means of communication available. The advent of the electric telegraph was a huge aid to efficient communication, but its operation was dependent upon telegraph clerks, and the first and last stage of every message was a handwritten piece of paper. Very large amounts of information needed to be recorded and circulated, with complex systems necessary to secure the uniformity necessary for efficiency. Nowadays, it is often said that paperwork systems, known rather disparagingly as 'bureaucracy', were invented by the Civil Service. Not so – the railways were first in the field. A large part of the collection consists of paper-based items, from single sheets to large casebound books. These were commonly referred to as 'ledgers' but were often not necessarily concerned with accounting.

The clerks were the nerves of the railway, with many specialties within the overall group. They provided communications without which the company could not function. Chief clerks were highly respected senior members of staff.

The most senior of uniformed staff were the stationmasters. A photograph of one such unidentified person is included here. The band on the straight-sided cap would be in either gilt or silver, depending on grade; it is not possible to tell which version is present in this

Left: A Midland Railway stationmaster.

Above Right: A stationmaster's cap.

Below Right: A later military-style cap.

instance. However, a cap in the collection has the gilt band. Towards the end of its existence (the precise date is unknown), the company introduced a military style of uniform cap. It is believed this was not introduced for stationmasters until after the Grouping.

A photograph of a young 'lad' (see p. 58), probably just starting his employment on the Midland, is notable for the disparity between the quality and appearance of the lad's corduroy uniform and that of the stationmaster, which is very evident. However, the lad was probably very proud of being a young railwayman.

The Midland encouraged their employees to undertake training in first aid and established an ambulance corps in association with the St John Ambulance, with regular training and proficiency examinations under the auspices of local doctors. Many aspects of outdoor railway work were inherently dangerous and, in the event of accidents, there were no emergency services as we know them today. Doctors often either had to walk or travel on horseback over quite long distances to treat injuries, and getting injured people to hospital could be a protracted business. In these circumstances early application of first aid was often vital to saving a life.

A selection of badges from the collection is shown. At the top is a cap badge from the Swansea Vale Railway, one of the constituent companies of the Midland, which was acquired in 1876. Left- and right-facing wyverns were used on a number of uniforms. These are shown together with nickel and gilt rope script MR badges. The larger of the two 'M' cap badges surmounted by wyverns is that of a senior inspector, while the smaller is that of a junior inspector. The two designs of Midland war service badges are shown together with a Marine Department ship's officer's cap badge. The lower 'MR-numeral' combination in nickel was worn by policemen on the tunic collar and by foremen on their jacket lapels.

Examples of Midland uniform buttons. Standard issue types: early 'coat of arms' (A, B) and later the common 'wyvern' (D). Departmental types: Hotel (E, F, H), Dining Car (K), Marine (J) and Police (L), together with LT&SR (C) and NCC (G) examples.

Left: Portrait of a 'lad' – probably a newly employed junior porter.

Below: Ambulance corps badges.

Ambulance medals (gold, silver and bronze).

Those qualified to administer first aid wore Midland Ambulance Corps badges on their uniforms; five different versions are shown on p. 58. The company also awarded certificates and medals in recognition of skilled first aid work at the scenes of accidents. The level of skill deployed was recognised by three different types of medals: gold, silver and bronze (see p. 59).

Ambulance boxes containing first aid equipment were located at strategic sites all over the system. Early boxes were wooden, while the later boxes were larger and of metal. The official contents list for one of these boxes is reproduced opposite.

Two complete uniforms are illustrated: one is that of a Midland ticket examiner (opposite) while the other is that of a tram driver on the Burton & Ashby Light Railways, which belonged to R. J. Shipton (see p. 62). A photograph of this gentleman wearing the uniform is included on p. 62. Although the tunic bears LMS insignia, it is believed to be an original Midland uniform.

Policemen were employed by railway companies from the very early days. The earliest police item in the collection is an Inspector's tipstaff from the Birmingham & Derby Junction Railway – one of the original three constituents of the Midland Railway. The tipstaff is hollow, and contained the warrant giving the inspector authority to make arrests. The procedure was to tap the person to be arrested on the shoulder with the staff – hence 'tipstaff.'

The standard work by Froggatt on railway uniforms (see bibliography) describes only one Midland type of police uniform, including a belt and the well-known traditional helmet. There is photographic evidence of three other types of uniform. One of those illustrated on p. 64 is particularly interesting because the name of the individual is recorded as Detective James R. Gates; it is assumed he was wearing his full dress uniform for a special occasion whereas normally he would be in plain clothes on duty.

Left: Early wooden ambulance box.

Right: Metal ambulance box.

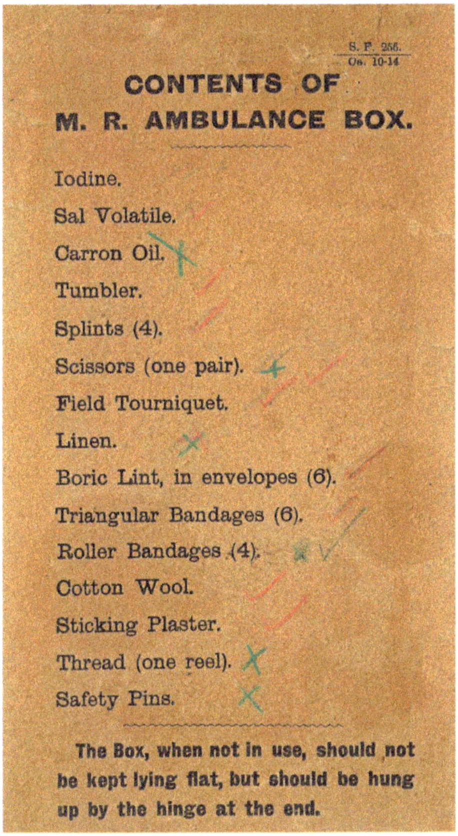

S. F. 256.
Os. 10-14

CONTENTS OF
M. R. AMBULANCE BOX.

Iodine.
Sal Volatile.
Carron Oil.
Tumbler.
Splints (4).
Scissors (one pair).
Field Tourniquet.
Linen.
Boric Lint, in envelopes (6).
Triangular Bandages (6).
Roller Bandages (4).
Cotton Wool.
Sticking Plaster.
Thread (one reel).
Safety Pins.

The Box, when not in use, should not be kept lying flat, but should be hung up by the hinge at the end.

Left: Ambulance box contents list.

Right: Ticket examiner's uniform.

Whistles were standard issue to many grades of staff, as were pocket watches to guards of both passenger and goods trains.

Discipline was strict – even harsh – by present day standards, with the threat of dismissal very real. Nevertheless, a 'job on the railway' was sought after and there were opportunities for promotion and regular wage reviews. (Evidence of these regular reviews is present in the collection with over 1,000 documents covering staff at Burton-on-Trent from 1869 to 1909.) The stability of the railways as an industry did literally provide the opportunity of 'jobs for life' and there were many long-service employees. One particular employee in the Carriage & Wagon Department worked for the company for seventy-two years. Newton Hibbert began his employment in 1849, aged thirteen, and died in service in 1921. A bronze plaque was erected in his memory, which is now in the collection.

The company provided support, both financial and otherwise, for a wide range of social facilities, and also welfare benefits for staff that, in many ways, were ahead of their time in Victorian England. Some examples of memorabilia from social activities sponsored by the company are shown on pp. 66–7.

Left: B&ALR tram driver's uniform, originally belonging to R. L. Shipton.

Right: R. L. Shipton is the driver of this B&ALR tram.

Police inspector's tipstaff, Birmingham & Derby Junction Railway.

Left: Three early (pre-1844) railway police truncheons of constituent MR companies: left to right, Birmingham and Gloucester, Midland Counties and Birmingham & Derby Junction railways.

Right: Traditional later pattern MR police helmet.

The MR policeman on duty in this photograph is overwhelmed by the magnificent gates at St Pancras (rarely photographed in the closed position); he is wearing the early pattern of helmet.

Left: MR policeman in a uniform cap not noted by Froggatt.

Right: MR full dress police uniform (Detective J. R. Gates).

A selection of MR whistles, including two traditionally shaped police issue. Others of the classic 'Thunderer' type include, top left, a Burton & Ashby Light Railways example, while top right is a Permanent Way Department issue. Two examples of whistles made with uniform buttons attached to the sides of the barrels are also shown.

Three MR guards' pocket watches, with faces marked 'MIDLAND'. The top example is an early key-wound watch with its brass key below.

Bronze plaque recording the long service of Newton Hibbert.

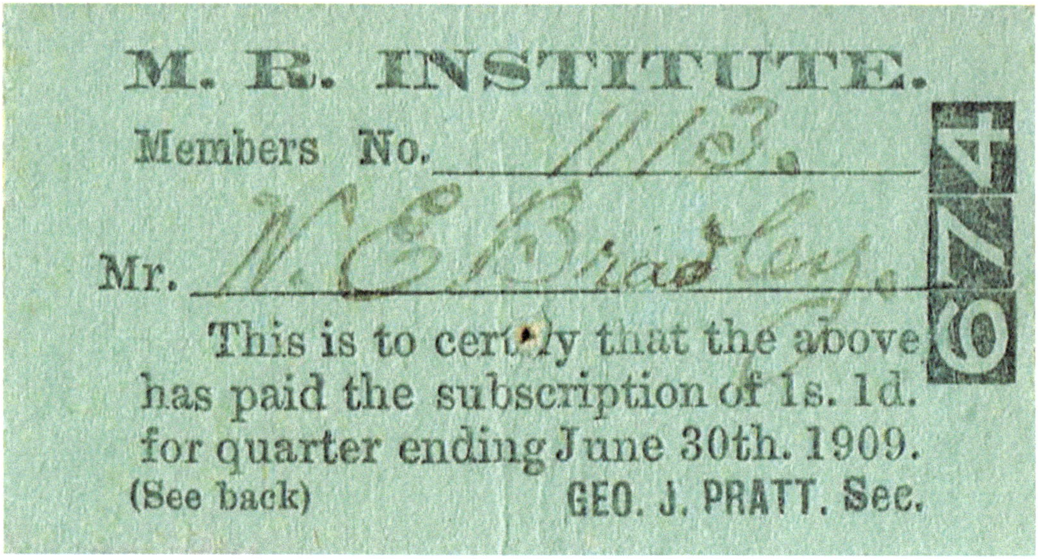

M. R. INSTITUTE.

Members No. 1113.

Mr. W. E. Bradley.

This is to certify that the above has paid the subscription of 1s. 1d. for quarter ending June 30th. 1909.

(See back) GEO. J. PRATT. Sec.

Membership ticket (in the form of a standard Edmondson card) for the Midland Railway Institute, which, in effect, was a social club open to all grades of employees. The facilities included a theatre, restaurant and library in a building purpose built by the company.

Hallmarked MR silver medal for interdepartmental football used after the Grouping by the Midland Division of the LMS.

Right: Two examples of annually awarded MR Rifle Club medals.

Below: MR Rifle Club ammunition ticket. This takes the form of a standard Edmondson card.

MIDLAND RAILWAY
OFFICERS' ANNUAL BALL,
Royal Drill Hall, Derby,
Friday, Feb. 6th, 1920

ARRANGEMENTS.

Accommodation at Midland Hotel and Station.

Two Dressing Rooms are provided in the Hotel, one for Ladies and one for Gentlemen.
The Station Refreshment Room, also Waiting Rooms for Ladies and Gentlemen, will be open on No. 1 platform on Saturday morning after the Ball for departing Guests.

Omnibuses.

Motor Omnibuses run between the Station, Midland Hotel, and Drill Hall, to convey Guests to and from the Ball. Distance one mile.

Cab Route.

All vehicles must enter Newland Street by way of Curzon Street or Abbey Street, and take up again in the same direction. Drivers should be instructed accordingly.

Cloak Rooms.

The Gentlemen's Cloak Room is situated at the entrance to the Hall in Newland Street.
Two Ladies' Cloak Rooms, up the steps leading from the Entrance Hall. The Stone Staircase is now entirely reserved for the use of Ladies.
Attendants take charge of all articles, and issue tickets for same.
A list of articles provided for the use of Guests is posted in each room.

General Office

Is situated just within the entrance to the Ball Room proper, where all matters relating to Programmes, Ball and Supper Tickets, Lost and Found Property, Letters, Telegrams, Time Tables, etc., are dealt with.

Ball Tickets.

Ball Tickets to be retained until entering Ball Room proper. Cases where tickets have been mislaid, or are not available for some other reason, to be referred to the Hon. Secretary.
Ladies should be accompanied into the Ball Room by a Gentleman.

Programmes.

Programmes are issued at the General Office to each Guest, and as the supply is regulated by the number of persons attending, it is hoped Visitors will endeavour to avoid the necessity of making a second application.
Guests are desired to insert their names in the space provided on the programme, in order to facilitate return should same be mislaid.
Enquiries in regard to lost or found programmes to be made at the General Office.

Supper Arrangements.

A coloured Supper Ticket is supplied with each Ball Ticket, and must be given up on entering the Supper Room.
The Suppers are timed as follows:—

Red Tickets	8.0 p.m.	Yellow Tickets	10.0 p.m.
Blue ,,	9.0 ,,	White ,,	11.30 ,,

Entrance to the Supper Room at 8.0, 9.0, and 10.0 p.m., is by a passage on the right-hand side facing the Refreshment Bar, leading direct from the Ball Room; the exit from the Supper Room being at the opposite corner to the left of the point of entrance, thence through the Reception Room into the Ball Room via the General Office.
For the Fourth Supper at 11.30 p.m., the method of entering and leaving the Supper Room is exactly reversed.
Anyone desirous of exchanging Supper Tickets for those of another colour should apply to the Assistant in charge of the General Office, who will endeavour to meet their wishes. After the Guests have been in the Supper Room 30 minutes a bell is rung to notify that the Supper Room must be cleared within 10 minutes from that time for relaying tables.
The times of the Suppers are shown on the Ball Programmes, and it is suggested that Guests erase the Dances taking place during the time they will be absent.
Oysters with Bread and Butter are provided during the whole of the night, in the small room at the end of the long Bar near the Supper Room exit.

Lounge and Smoke Rooms.

Access to the Balcony and Lounge is by way of the staircase leading from the Ball Room proper, near the General Office.
The Lounge is for Ladies and Gentlemen, and Smoking is permitted, but not Card Playing.
Gentlemen are requested to exercise every possible care in the use of matches, lighted cigars, or cigarettes, to prevent damage to the furniture, kindly lent for the occasion by Messrs. John Jones & Sons.
A waiter is in attendance to obtain refreshments. There is also a bar in the room adjoining, at which Coffee, Oysters, etc., are obtainable.
No Smoking is permitted on the Balcony.
Smoking in the Hall, anterooms, and approaches (other than in the rooms set apart) is strictly prohibited. Gentlemen are requested not to carry matches in their dress clothes.
Matches are provided gratis in each of the Smoke Rooms.

Licence.

The Liquor Control Regulations provide that there shall be no sale nor supply for consumption of intoxicating liquor at the Bars after 11.0 p.m.

Lavatories, &c.

The Gentlemen's Lavatory is reached by a passage near the end of the Bar furthest from the Ball Room entrance.
A Hairdresser is in attendance.
The Ladies' Retiring Rooms are on the left side of the stage looking towards the Bandstand (in one of which a Waitress is in attendance to obtain Refreshments), and Ladies' Cloak Rooms upstairs from Entrance Hall. A List of Articles provided for the use of Guests is posted in each room.

Articles Found.

Articles found should be taken to the Assistant in the General Office deputed to take charge of Lost Property, to whom all applications for their recovery are to be made. A Signature is required for property returned to the Owners.

Telegrams and Letters.

Addressed "c/o Mallory, Drill Hall, Derby," obtainable on application at the General Office.

Time Tables & Train Departure Lists

Provided at the above Office.

Officers.

The M.C., Committee, and Stewards wear distinctive badges.

Hon. Secretary's Office.

The Hon. Secretary's Office is in the Ball Room near to the Supper Room exit, and he will be prepared to deal with any complaints or difficulties which may arise during the night.

Dancing

From 7.30 p.m. to 4.30 a.m.

N.B.—All the facilities, *i.e.*, Omnibuses, Dressing, Cloak, Retiring and Smoke Rooms, Lavatories, and Attendances, enumerated on this card are provided free of charge.
Suggestions that will add to the comfort of the Guests will receive careful consideration.

FOR THE COMMITTEE,
Geo. G. Mallory, Hon. Sec.

Official arrangements for the 1920 officers' ball.

Four identification badges worn by officials at the officers' ball. In the early years these had cloth centres with tassels but they were later changed to enamelled gilt. Two examples of each are shown.

The Midland Railway officers' ball was a most prestigious social event and was held annually in the Royal Drill Hall in Derby every February from 1870 to 1923 (excluding the war years 1915 to 1919). Reproduced opposite in full are the arrangements for the 1920 ball. Not only do they give an idea of the scale of the event but, in their way, also offer a subtle commentary on 1920s society. The arrangements include a note that 'The MC, Committee and Stewards wear distinctive badges' (see above).

Chapter 4

Horses

Horses continued to be vital to the prosperity of the railways for over a century after stagecoach travel gave way to steam-hauled trains on iron rails. Their importance can be judged by considering a few statistics relating to the Midland Railway in 1914. The company owned 4,990 horses for road vehicle work and 160 specifically for shunting duties: a total of 5,150. This contrasts with a total locomotive stock of 3,066. The total number of horse-drawn road vehicles was 7,235 (including twenty-four horse omnibuses). By comparison their road motor vehicle stock was precisely twenty. This had risen to 171 by 1922, while the number of horses had reduced to 3,224. These two statistics illustrate the beginning of the trend that would see, over the following fifty years, the near-total dominance by the motor vehicle of overland freight transport. Horse-drawn drays, carts and vans owned by the railway companies were a common sight in the streets of cities, towns and larger villages throughout the UK in the nineteenth century, and continued in use until well after nationalisation in 1948. They provided the means whereby goods and parcels were delivered to customers from the nearest railway station: the all-important 'final mile'. In addition, horses were used for shunting rail vehicles in locations where it was not possible (or was uneconomical) to use steam locomotives.

Looking after such a large number of horses spread all over the country, from Carlisle in the north, to Swansea and Bristol in the south, and Southend in the east, was a major task, requiring the deployment of significant resources in the shape of the Horse Department, headed by the horse superintendent – part of the company's Goods Manager's organisation located in Derby. Possibly the first superintendent was a Mr Shepherd, who was replaced by J. E. Swallow in 1855 and, in turn, by William Feast upon Swallow's retirement in 1890. The *Derby Daily Telegraph* reported in 1924, on the occasion of Feast's retirement, that he had held responsibility for the purchase of all horses; selection as to appropriate work; and the inspection of studs and all harness and saddlery work at various saddlers' shops across the system after the work had been brought in-house from private contractors. He also had responsibility for overseeing the maintenance of horse-drawn vehicles by outside contractors, until that work too was brought in-house and became the responsibility of the Carriage & Wagon Department (at a so far unknown date).

This posed photograph (note the rear wheel chock) of a typical Midland Railway single horse dray is believed to have been taken in Cromford in the Derbyshire Peak District. It clearly shows the harness arrangements in everyday use for this type of haulage. This dray would have plied between Arkwright's Mill in Cromford and the railway station, carrying their products for despatch by rail. There is a note on the back of the photograph that the drayman's name was either a Mr Bonsall or Joe Pearson, both thought to be residents of Cromford.

This photograph shows a horse engaged on shunting duties at an unknown location. The vehicle it is about to move is Midland Railway horsebox No. 456, built in 1899. The photograph is therefore early twentieth century. Note the somewhat different harness arrangement for this duty compared with the Cromford photograph. (John Alsop)

Extensive stabling was required at the major goods stations such as St Pancras and Somerstown in London, Lawley Street in Birmingham and St Mary's in Derby. Stables were also provided at many other stations and these were often substantial buildings designed by the company's architect. An example is in the collection (unfortunately not suitable for reproduction) for a stable block of twenty stalls with two loose boxes and a three-bedroom cottage for the horsekeeper at Walsall in 1884.

Provision of feed for the horses located all over the Midland system was a major logistical task. Large provender stores were maintained by the company's Stores Department at Oakham and Ashchurch, from where regular deliveries of feed were made by rail to all the company's stables.

The Midland employed its own veterinary surgeons, based in Derby and London, and the bottle pictured on p. 73 would indicate that, organisationally, there was a Veterinary Department answerable directly to the goods manager, independently of the Horse Department. This tends to be confirmed by the chief veterinary surgeon's salary being more than twice that of the horse superintendent in 1906.

With over 5,000 horses, large quantities of harness were required and a number of examples of Midland Railway items have survived into the collection. These include a bridle, two saddles and a pair of hames (see pp. 74–5).

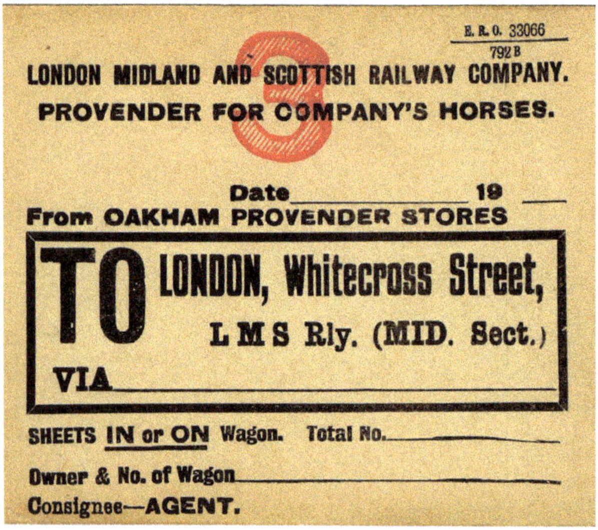

This LMS wagon label is basically a Midland Railway design and is pre-printed with essential details indicating a large regular usage. All wagons were individually labelled to show their destination and the route to be taken. The labels had to be able to be read by shunters on the ground in goods and marshalling yards, and so were placed at eye level in special holders either on the solebar or lower part of the wagon. In the case of the horse box on the previous page, the label is just visible in its special holder by the left shoulder of the gentleman in cap and riding breeches.

Another pre-printed label, this time of the tie-on type and of Midland Railway origin, for the return of a bundle of empty forage sacks to the Provender Store at Oakham (Mr Derry had succeeded Mr Morrall as the company's stores superintendent upon the latter's death in 1902).

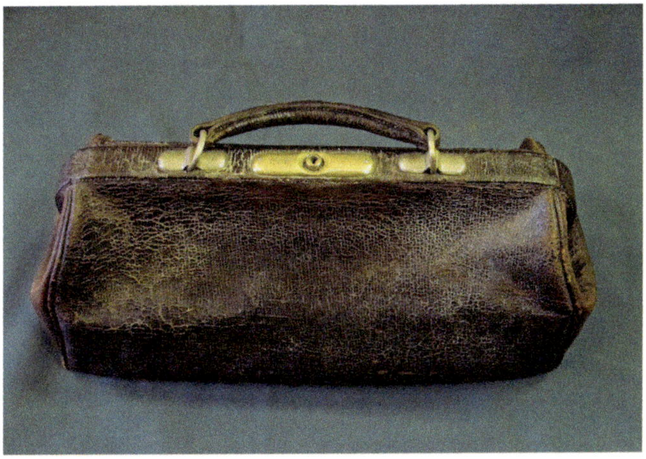

A veterinary surgeon's bag with the company's initials engraved on the brass lock. The tub of horse liniment was found inside the bag, thus tending to confirm its use by the veterinary surgeons.

A Veterinary Department bottle.

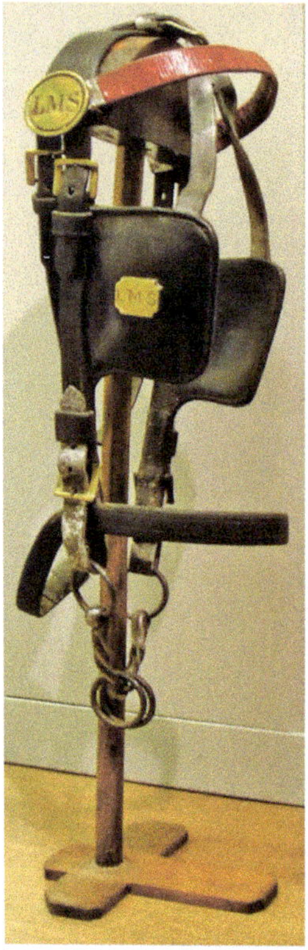

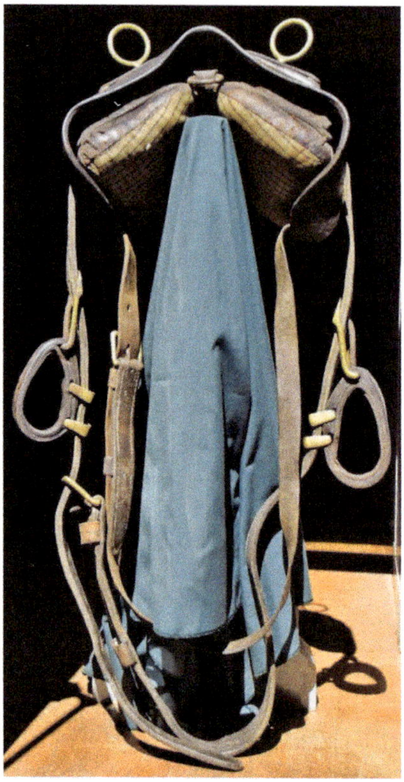

Three items of harness are shown in this illustration.

The brasses on the bridle (top left) indicate LMS ownership. In actual fact, the bridle is of Midland Railway origin, as the leather elements are stamped MRCo in several places. The rosettes and blinker brasses were replaced with LMS versions of the Midland standard sometime after the Grouping, and should be compared with items (E) and (H) shown in the illustration on p. 76. The browband is coloured red, which was a common feature for horses working in London.

Top right is the smaller of the two saddles in the collection, arranged to show the associated girth straps and buckles. Note the loops on each side, which supported the cart shafts. This design of saddle was used by smaller horses hauling lighter loads.

The lower picture shows a pair of hames, which were fitted one on each side of the horse collar and are clearly shown in the images on p. 71. The rings were used in some hames configurations to guide the leading reins from the bridle to the driver sitting on the front of the dray. These examples are basically made from cast iron and are brass plated. They are stamped M.R.Co.

This view of the heavy-duty saddle in the collection shows the positions of the four rectangular saddle brasses, which were fixed on most Midland saddles. However, in a small number of cases, they could vary in terms of the size and style of the engraved letters; even a round version is known – see (i) below.

A selection of four brass hubcaps (from the eight in the collection) for use on horse-drawn drays and vans. Designs were all similar but many different markings were used; the variations often arose when the drays were built by contractors who engraved their name as well as the initials of the company. Hubcaps took a lot of bumps and knocks during use and the resulting marks are clearly visible.

It had been traditional practice for very many years before the railway era to decorate the harness with small, simply shaped brasses, e.g., rectangles or ovals. From 1850 onwards it became the norm to extend harness decorations for the heavy horse, using more complex brasses, and one very popular trend was to use designs incorporating the names or initials of owners. The railways used such brasses extensively. A booklet by the late Ran Hawthorne, published in 1987 (see bibliography), summarised all the railway horse brasses known at the time, which had become very collectable items. Included here is a view of a near full set of Midland Railway horse brasses from the collection, mounted on a display board. There are essentially five generic types of brasses represented. These are:

(i) Harness decorations distinguished by the use of integrally cast brass prongs to attach the brass to the harness leather. There are six examples on the board. The most common is the small rectangular brass with scalloped corners (E) (1.7 x 1.4 in.). It was used on saddles and blinkers. There is a slightly larger brass of similar proportions (J) (2.5 x 2.0 in.) and two of differing proportions (C) (1.6 x 1.9 in.) and (K) (2.4 x 2.15 in.). Both are quite rare, while the circular example (F) (2.2 in. diameter) is also rare and is claimed by Hawthorne to be 'the only known circular railway harness decoration which has prongs on the back for fixing and is not to be confused with a rosette'. Example (D) is not mentioned by Hawthorne.

The Society's collection of horse brasses.

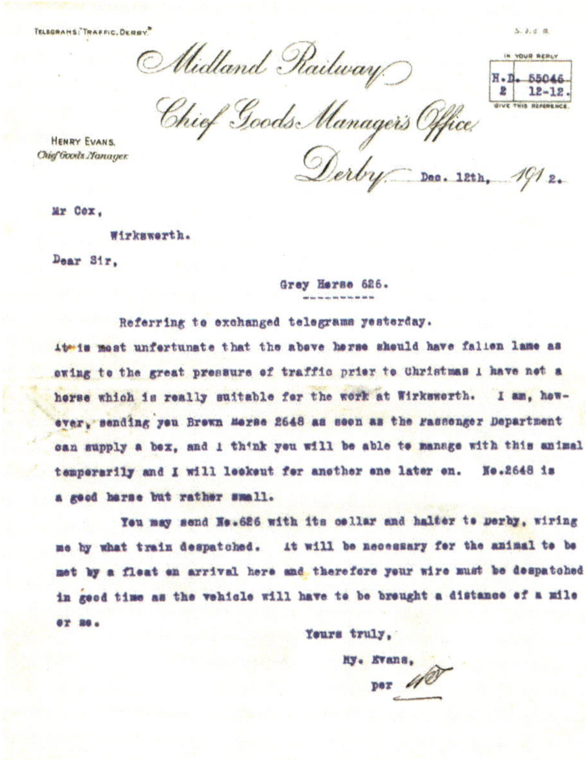

TELEGRAMS: "TRAFFIC, DERBY."

IN YOUR REPLY H.D. 55046. 2 12-12. GIVE THIS REFERENCE.

Midland Railway

Chief Goods Manager's Office

HENRY EVANS.
Chief Goods Manager.

Derby Dec. 12th, 1912.

Mr Cox,

Wirksworth.

Dear Sir,

Grey Horse 626.

Referring to exchanged telegrams yesterday.
It is most unfortunate that the above horse should have fallen lame as owing to the great pressure of traffic prior to Christmas I have not a horse which is really suitable for the work at Wirksworth. I am, however, sending you Brown Horse 2648 as soon as the Passenger Department can supply a box, and I think you will be able to manage with this animal temporarily and I will lookout for another one later on. No.2648 is a good horse but rather small.

You may send No.626 with its collar and halter to Derby, wiring me by what train despatched. It will be necessary for the animal to be met by a float on arrival here and therefore your wire must be despatched in good time as the vehicle will have to be brought a distance of a mile or so.

Yours truly,

Hy. Evans,

per

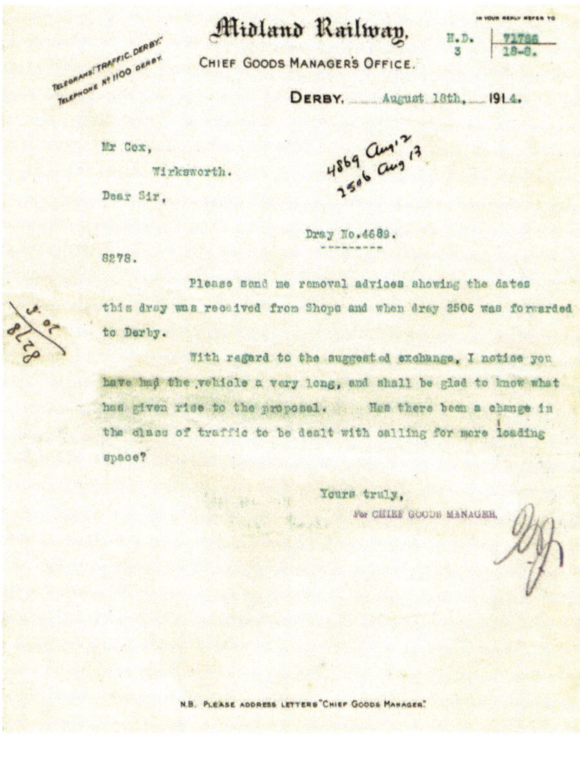

Midland Railway.

CHIEF GOODS MANAGER'S OFFICE.

IN YOUR REPLY REFER TO H.D. 3 71786 18-8.

TELEGRAMS: "TRAFFIC, DERBY." TELEPHONE Nº 1100 DERBY.

DERBY, August 18th, 1914.

Mr Cox,

Wirksworth.

4869 Aug 12
2506 Aug 17

Dear Sir,

Dray No.4689.

8278.

Please send me removal advices showing the dates this dray was received from Shops and when dray 2506 was forwarded to Derby.

With regard to the suggested exchange, I notice you have had the vehicle a very long, and shall be glad to know what has given rise to the proposal. Has there been a change in the class of traffic to be dealt with calling for more loading space?

Yours truly,

For CHIEF GOODS MANAGER.

N.B. PLEASE ADDRESS LETTERS "CHIEF GOODS MANAGER."

Two internal letters from the Horse Department illustrating different tasks involved in looking after the company's horses. Other subjects covered by similar letters in the collection include arrangements for winter shoeing, clipping and singeing of horses.

How there came to be so many variants is not known, but it is probably due to the different contractors who manufactured the company's saddlery before the work was brought in-house being allowed some latitude in the design of the relevant brasses. When the company took direct control of manufacturing, it would have been much easier to enforce standardisation, which would also account for the relatively high survival rate of the small rectangular version (E).

(ii) Hanging brasses normally attached to the harness by a horizontal loop or bar at the top of the brass. Item L is one of two Midland designs listed by Hawthorne. It would have been mounted on a leather facepiece fixed to the bridle browband. The second design (not in the collection) is adapted from the rosette (H) by the addition of a hanging bar at the top.

(iii) Rosette worn one on each side of the bridle where the two top leathers (the crownband and browband) meet. Two variants of the rosette are known: examples (H) and (G). The former has a diameter of 2.55 inches, while the latter is smaller (2.25 inches diameter) and made of thinner brass, with the letters infilled red. It is believed that the smaller rosettes were fitted to bridles of smaller horses used to pull lighter vehicles.

(iv) Hameplate, which is mounted on a leather strap between the tops of the hames. Hawthorne does not list any specific Midland Railway hameplates but the collection has two: (B) and (M). The former is clearly made up locally using the standard rectangular harness decoration on a brass plate of similar outline shape to (M). This latter is believed to be the standard issued by the Midland, but probably in small quantities.

(v) A swinger that, in the case of the Midland, consists of a round hinged disc within a circular frame (A), which, in turn, is mounted on the crownband (top) of the bridle. Swingers are not listed by Hawthorne for any pre- or post-Grouping railway.

Photographic evidence suggests that hanging brasses, hameplates and swingers were not usually fitted to harnesses in everyday use. Railway horses did take part in regular local parades, and it is likely that these more decorative brasses were only used on such occasions when an immaculate turnout of both horse and dray was obligatory. It is these local events that could have given rise to locally produced brasses not formally issued by the company. In particular, photographic evidence is needed to establish beyond doubt the use in Midland Railway days of the swinger in the collection.

There were a multitude of tasks involved in the administration of the Horse Department. Two internal letters from Headquarters in Derby, addressed to Mr Cox (the stationmaster at Wirksworth) and now in the collection, give a flavour of the diverse nature of routine work involved in looking after the horse population. Another letter in the collection, again from Headquarters but this time to Settle and dated January 1879, concerns the sale of manure. It confirms that the prices to be charged are 2*s* 6*d* per horse per month for stable manure and 1*s* 8*d* per month for 'yard sweepings'.

An appropriate way to close this chapter is to illustrate an oil lamp used as a red rear light on a horse-drawn cart or dray.

A rear light for a horse-drawn road vehicle.

CHAPTER 5

Hotels and Catering

In 1864, a boy of fifteen named William Towle joined the Midland Railway as an assistant in the Midland Hotel in Derby. At the age of twenty-two, he was appointed manager. Thus began a 150-year Towle family dynasty in the service of the hotel and catering industry in the UK. Under William's leadership the Midland led the way in the development of the railway hotel and catering business during the Victorian

Three Midland hotels illustrated by means of postcards from the collection. The first two of the Adephi in Liverpool before and after the rebuilding are cards officially issued by the company. The third, of the Midland Manchester, is a card by Tuck.

and Edwardian periods. It had acquired the Station Hotel at Normanton in 1861, the Midland in Derby in 1862 and the Queens in Leeds in 1863, which was subsequently enlarged in 1867 and 1898. It took over the North Western Hotel in Morecambe in 1871; this was immediately renamed the Midland Hotel. In 1873 it opened the prestigious Midland Grand Hotel in London, designed by Sir George Gilbert Scott; it still forms the magnificent façade to complement Barlow's pioneering arched roof at St Pancras station.

The Midland continued to invest heavily to create a chain of railway hotels second to none. It opened the Midland Hotel in Bradford in 1890 and went on to build a major new hotel in Manchester – again called the Midland – which opened in 1903. Charles Trubshaw, the company's architect, was responsible for the design of both.

Two smaller hotels were acquired in the meantime: Heysham Towers (near Morecambe) in 1896 and the Queens in Keighley in 1902. The final investment by the company in a large prestigious hotel was the complete rebuilding and refurbishment in 1912–14 of the Adelphi in Liverpool, which it had purchased in 1892.

William Towle retired in 1914, whereupon his two sons, Francis and Arthur, were appointed to succeed him as joint managers. They had both joined the Midland Hotels Department in 1896 under their father and went on to become successful leading national figures in the hotel and catering profession in the inter-war years, according to Oliver Carter (*An Illustrated History of British Railway Hotels 1838–1983*, see bibliography). Francis was honoured with a knighthood in 1919, as was his father William in 1920. For some reason, on internal documents (e.g., board minutes) Francis was referred to as Frank; this name was also used externally on official postcards.

Many of the artefacts and documents from the Midland Hotels Department that have survived reflect the custom and practice of the Victorian era. The most visually striking derive from the large quantities of silver plate and china, which were often specially

This illustration is of an advertising enamel featuring two of the Midland hotels in Leeds and Bradford. This enamel was unusual at the time in featuring photographic images and was one of a group of enamels illustrating its hotels that the Midland produced to be assembled at suitable locations in a wooden framework to present a large advertisement hoarding.

designed and procured for use in the largest and most prestigious of the company's hotels – particularly so in the case of the Midland Grand.

The Society has over 750 different items of hotel and catering china, silver plate and glassware. In addition, there are over 2,300 archive documents in the collection relating to the management of the company's Hotels Department.

En suite facilities were not a feature of Victorian hotels; pictured is a contemporary photograph of a bedroom in the Adelphi Hotel in Liverpool, where washing facilities consisted of two pairs of wash bowls and water ewers. A similar pair are held in the collection (see opposite). These are of a relatively plain design and bear the standard MRH (Midland Railway Hotels) script letter emblem. They would have been used in any of the company's hotels.

Other bedroom china included slop pails, whose purpose was to receive the contents of the wash basin after use. Chamber pots were essential in every bedroom and the design of these varied widely. A selection of four is shown on p. 84, including the highly decorated example by Royal Worcester from the Midland Grand. Including as it does a significant amount of gold leaf, it is certainly a candidate to be accorded the title of the most highly decorated piece of railway china. Special designs of china were created for the more important hotels, particularly the Midland Grand, where bedroom china appears to have received special attention. It is likely that separate designs were created for use in differently priced rooms or suites, with the more ornate being allocated to the higher

A table place setting formed of selected items from the collection.

A bedroom in the Adelphi Hotel in Liverpool during Midland Railway days.

A wash bowl and water ewer similar to the ones in the above photograph.

A selection of Midland Railway chamber pots from the eight in the collection.

A slop pail, footbath and chamber pot from the Midland Grand.

Six examples of silver plate from the collection:

An asparagus dish with sauce boat by Elkington, each bearing the wyvern/Midland Hotels emblem.

A small fluted pedestal bowl bearing the Midland Grand banner emblem.

A fruit bowl by Elkington bearing the wyvern/Midland Grand emblem engraved in the centre.

A small plain bowl showing the Midland Hotel Derby circular garter emblem.

A pair of nutcrackers bearing the Midland Grand banner emblem.

A latticed dish bearing the wyvern/Midland Hotels emblem.

Four further examples of silver plate from the collection:

A hinged-lid hot water jug by Mappin & Webb's (*sic*) bearing the Midland Steamers laurel wreath emblem.

A sugar sifter bearing the Midland Hotels laurel wreath emblem.

A pepper mill by Mappin & Webb's (*sic*), engraved 'MIDLAND HOTELS' around the base.

A silver gilt table candelabra by Elkington bearing the wyvern/Midland Hotels emblem on the base.

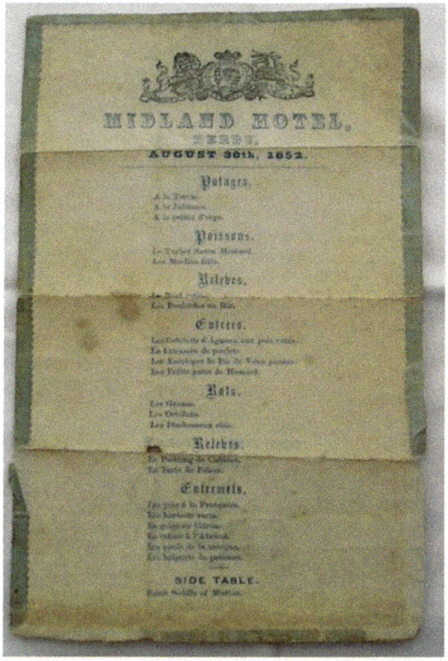

Queen Victoria was a regular user of the railways when travelling in the UK and Derby was an appropriate location to break some of her longer journeys. She and her suite would stay overnight at the Midland Hotel, which was very convenient being so close to the station. The menu illustrated is printed on silk and was for dinner on the evening of 30 August 1852, during one of her overnight stops. It is believed that use of the hotel by the Queen led to the approval to incorporate the crown into a design of emblem used on the hotel's china, which simply read 'The Midland', with no mention of hotel or Derby (see cup and saucer illustrated).

The silver-plate cake stand is engraved 'MIDLAND HOTEL DERBY' around the vertical circumference of the ornate base.

The hotel's extended basement incorporated the company's bottling stores. Illustrated is a brandy flask that, very unusually, has survived complete with label. The main activity of the stores was, however, the bottling of beer. Many variations of glass bottles were used over the years, with both clear glass and many shades of green. The collection has twenty-three such examples.

priced accommodation. Pictured on p. 84 are two different designs for the Midland Grand: a slop pail and two items of matching design, a footbath and chamber pot.

In the pre-Grouping era, smoking was not the anti-social habit it has now become 100 years later – quite the reverse in fact, as cigarette smoking in particular was considered one of the heights of fashionable behaviour. The manufacturers of tobacco products were keen to join with the larger hotels to exploit the hotel guest market. The ancillary device essential to the smoker was the match, and again the manufacturers supported the hotels by providing small containers (vesta tins) of matches specially printed to publicise the hotels concerned. Vesta tins (and their matches) were smaller than the standard 'England's Glory' matchbox (1.8 x 1.3 x 0.5 inches compared with 2.1 x 1.5 x 0.75 inches) and more conveniently fitted in the waistcoat pocket. The presence of the royal coat of arms on the H. L. Savoury cigarette boxes probably added an implied note of social approval to the habit.

Smokers' products produced for Midland hotels.

In 1884 William Towle assumed responsibility for station refreshment rooms and the operation of dining cars in addition to hotels. By this time he had moved his headquarters from Derby to the Midland Grand at St Pancras and thus the Hotels Department became the only major department of the company to be 'headquartered' away from Derby.

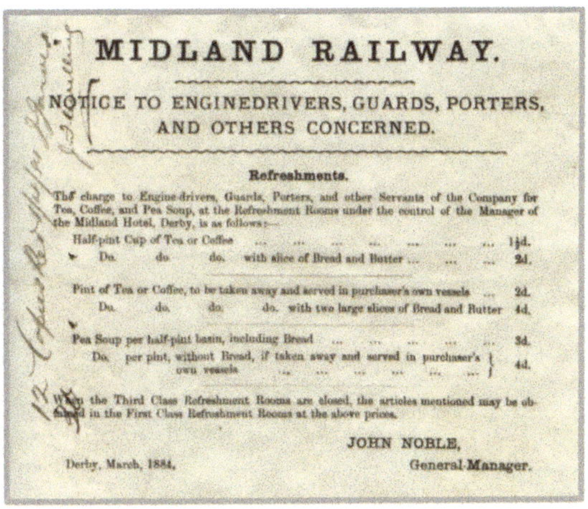

MIDLAND RAILWAY.

NOTICE TO ENGINEDRIVERS, GUARDS, PORTERS, AND OTHERS CONCERNED.

Refreshments.

The charge to Engine-drivers, Guards, Porters, and other Servants of the Company for Tea, Coffee, and Pea Soup, at the Refreshment Rooms under the control of the Manager of the Midland Hotel, Derby, is as follows:—

Half-pint Cup of Tea or Coffee ... ... 1½d.
Do. do. do. with slice of Bread and Butter ... ... 2d.

Pint of Tea or Coffee, to be taken away and served in purchaser's own vessels ... 2d.
Do. do. do. do. with two large slices of Bread and Butter 4d.

Pea Soup per half-pint basin, including Bread ... ... 3d.
Do. per pint, without Bread, if taken away and served in purchaser's own vessels ... ... 4d.

When the Third Class Refreshment Rooms are closed, the articles mentioned may be obtained in the First Class Refreshment Rooms at the above prices.

JOHN NOBLE,
General Manager.

Derby, March, 1884.

A refreshment room miscellany.

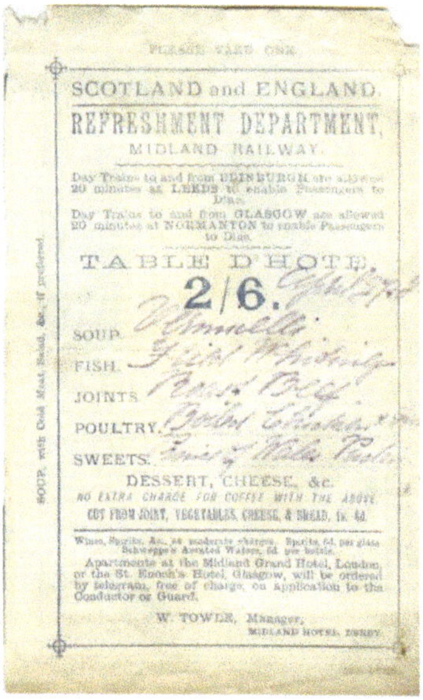

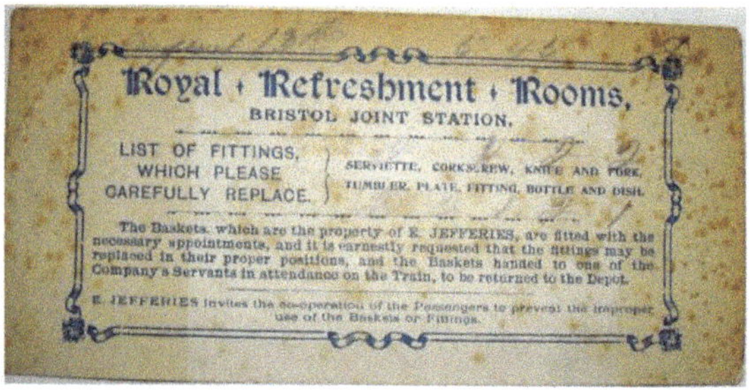

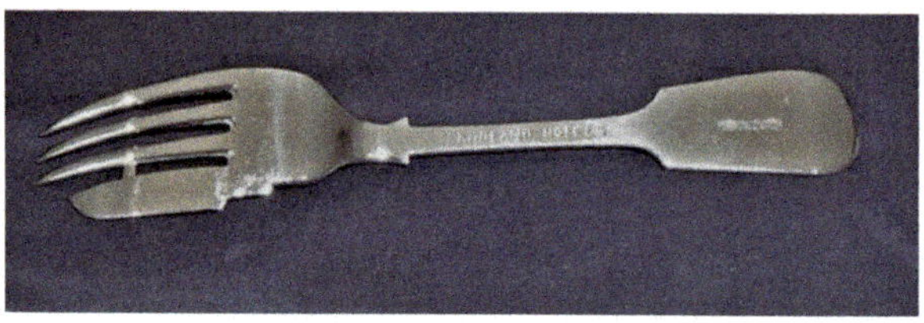

A further refreshment room miscellany.

An example of Midland Railway glassware for use in dining cars, featuring the 'Midland Cars' laurel wreath emblem.

Refreshment room china and, in some cases, items of silver plate were often specially marked with their own emblems (including locations). Similar arrangements were made to identify tableware to be used in dining cars.

Before the advent of corridor trains, which made dining cars a practical proposition, the company sought to provide refreshments and food for its long-distance passengers by stopping its principal Anglo-Scottish express trains for twenty to thirty minutes at a convenient station with dining facilities at roughly the mid-point of the journey. Two such stations used for this purpose were Normanton and Leeds (Wellington). One particular example was the northbound 9.45 a.m. express from St Pancras to Glasgow, which called at Normanton for twenty minutes from 1.28 p.m. to 1.48 p.m. Menus were available on the train and passengers could make their selection to be handed to station staff during an earlier stop – Leicester in this case. Details were then telegraphed forward to Normanton so that the food would be ready to be served in the dining room on the station immediately on arrival.

Luncheon baskets were provided at major stations and the refreshment trolley illustrated on p. 93 shows one with an enamel plate lettered 'M R Derby' (arrowed), indicating the station

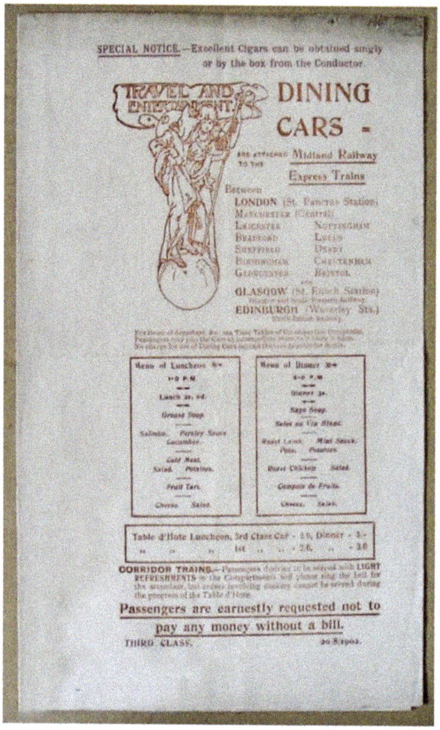
SPECIAL NOTICE.—Excellent Cigars can be obtained singly or by the box from the Conductor.

DINING CARS

are attached to the Midland Railway Express Trains

Between

LONDON (St. Pancras Station)

MANCHESTER (Central)

LEICESTER NOTTINGHAM

BRADFORD LEEDS

SHEFFIELD DERBY

BIRMINGHAM CHELTENHAM

GLOUCESTER BRISTOL

and

GLASGOW (St. Enoch Station)

EDINBURGH (Waverley Stn.)

Menu of Luncheon	Menu of Dinner
Lunch 2s. 6d.	Dinner 3s.
Grouse Soup	Sago Soup
Salmon. Parsley Sauce. Cucumber.	Soles au Vin Blanc
Cold Meat. Salad. Potatoes.	Roast Lamb. Mint Sauce. Peas. Potatoes.
Fruit Tart.	Roast Chicken. Salad.
Cheese. Salad.	Compote de Fruits.
	Cheese. Salad.

Table d'Hote Luncheon, 3rd Class Car - 2/0, Dinner - 2/-
„ „ „ 1st „ „ - 2/6, „ - 3/0

CORRIDOR TRAINS.—Passengers desiring to be served with LIGHT REFRESHMENTS in the Compartments will please ring the bell for the attendant, but orders involving cooking cannot be served during the progress of the Table d'Hote.

Passengers are earnestly requested not to pay any money without a bill.

THIRD CLASS. 20/8/1902.

MENU OF LUNCHEON 2/6	MENU OF DINNER 3/-
Portugaise.	Mutton Broth.
Fried Sole. Anchovy Sauce.	Halibut. Parsley Sauce.
Roast Beef. Beans. Potatoes.	Poulet Sauté aux Champignons.
Fruit Tart.	Roast Mutton. Cabbage. Potatoes.
Cheese. Salad.	Savarins aux Liqueurs.
	Cheese. Salad.

CAR 14

THIRD CLASS. 24 8 1904.

MIDLAND RAILWAY DINING CARS

PASSENGERS ARE EARNESTLY REQUESTED NOT TO PAY ANY MONEY WITHOUT A BILL; AND TO FORWARD COMPLAINTS OR SUGGESTIONS TO WM TOWLE, ST PANCRAS HOTEL, LONDON, N.W.

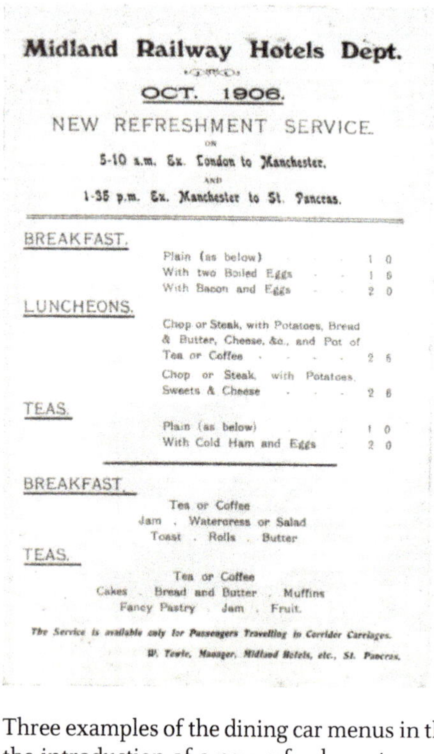
Midland Railway Hotels Dept.

OCT. 1906.

NEW REFRESHMENT SERVICE

ON

5-10 a.m. Ex. London to Manchester,

AND

1-35 p.m. Ex. Manchester to St. Pancras.

BREAKFAST.	Plain (as below)	1 0
	With two Boiled Eggs	1 6
	With Bacon and Eggs	2 0
LUNCHEONS.	Chop or Steak, with Potatoes, Bread & Butter, Cheese, &c., and Pot of Tea or Coffee	2 6
	Chop or Steak, with Potatoes, Sweets & Cheese	2 6
TEAS.	Plain (as below)	1 0
	With Cold Ham and Eggs	2 0

BREAKFAST.

Tea or Coffee

Jam . Watercress or Salad

Toast . Rolls . Butter

TEAS.

Tea or Coffee

Cakes . Bread and Butter . Muffins

Fancy Pastry . Jam . Fruit.

The Service is available only for Passengers Travelling in Corridor Carriages.

W. Towle, Manager, Midland Hotels, etc., St. Pancras.

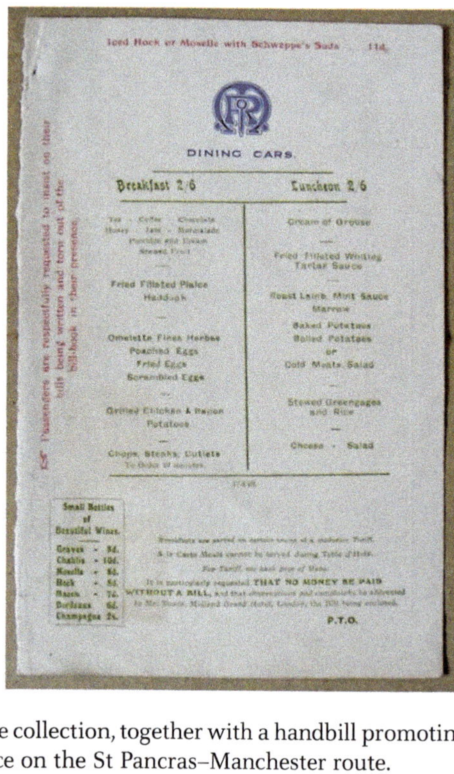
Iced Hock or Moselle with Schweppe's Soda 1/4

DINING CARS.

Breakfast 2/6	Luncheon 2/6
Fried Filleted Plaice. Haddock	Cream of Grouse
Omelette Fines Herbes. Poached Eggs. Fried Eggs. Scrambled Eggs	Fried Filleted Whiting. Tartar Sauce
Grilled Chicken & Bacon. Potatoes	Roast Lamb. Mint Sauce. Marrow. Baked Potatoes. Boiled Potatoes or Cold Meats. Salad
Chops, Steaks, Cutlets	Stewed Greengages and Rice
	Cheese - Salad

Small Bottles of Beautiful Wines.

Graves - 8d.
Chablis - 10d.
Moselle - 8d.
Hock - 8d.
Macon - 7d.
Bordeaux 6d.
Champagne 2s.

THAT NO MONEY BE PAID WITHOUT A BILL,

P.T.O.

Passengers are respectfully requested to insist on their bills being written and torn out of the bill-book in their presence.

Three examples of the dining car menus in the collection, together with a handbill promoting the introduction of a new refreshment service on the St Pancras–Manchester route.

Midland Railway refreshment trolley, photographed on Platform 1 at Derby.

to which it should be returned after use. An actual example of the plate is in the Collection and illustrated on p. 90. The leaflet also illustrated, also on p. 90, indicates that the provision of luncheon baskets at Bristol Joint Station was subcontracted to a Mr E. Jefferies, who no doubt supplied them both to Great Western and Midland passengers. The copper urn in the collection is similar to that shown as part of the equipment on the trolley.

Two unusual items also illustrated on p. 90 are a badge worn by staff (almost certainly volunteers) serving at a special soldiers' and sailors' buffet (S&SB) on Sheffield station during the First World War. The fork, with an enlarged prong, sharpened along one edge to use as a knife, is believed to have been introduced for use by servicemen who had been injured in combat and lost an arm as a result. It bears the mark MIDLAND HOTELS.

A book was published by the author at the time of MR 150 (see Introduction) which includes comprehensive illustrations of the emblems and marks to be found on Midland Railway china, silverplate and cutlery (see Bibliography).

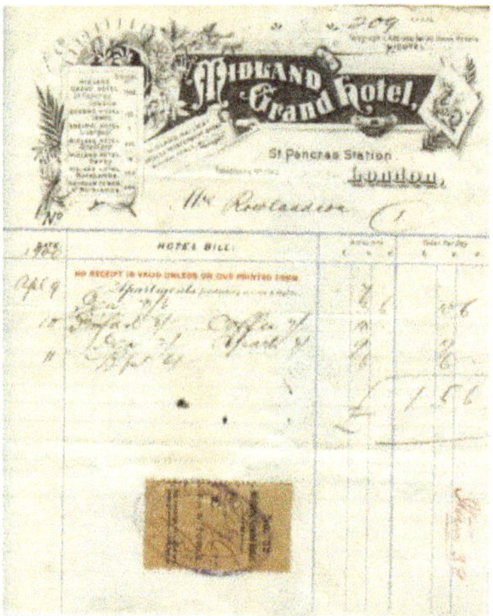

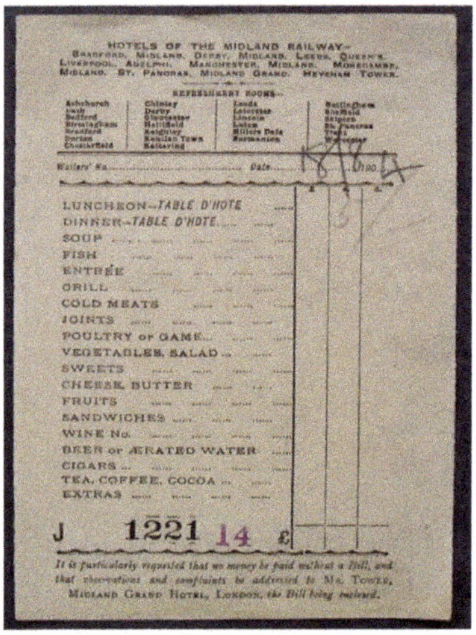

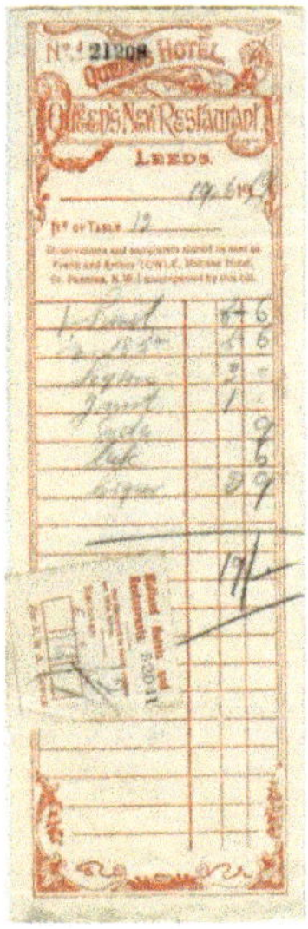

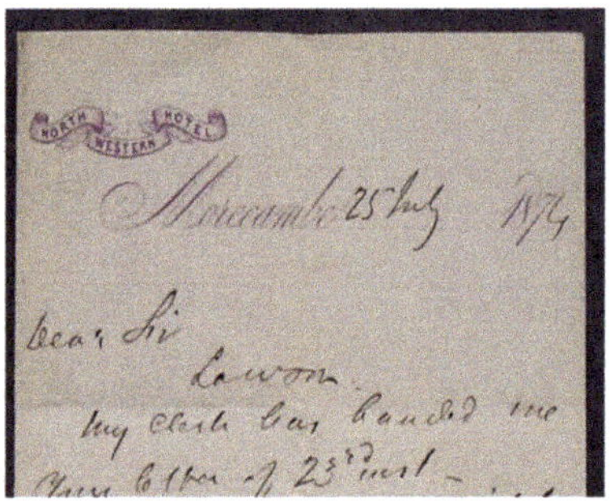

Examples of Midland Railway Hotels Department printed material. Three different patterns of bills and receipts are shown, together with an unusual railway rule book. The Adelphi Hotel item is an oval gummed luggage label. The letterhead from the North Western Hotel Morecambe is dated 25 July 1874 – three years after it was renamed 'The Midland' following amalgamation.

Dedication – to Fred Gray

This book is dedicated to Fred Gray. Fred is a railway enthusiast from the pre-war era. Aged seventeen when war broke out, he served in the Army and, upon return, became committed to the cause of railway preservation during the brutalism of the Beeching era. He was particularly concerned to ensure that it wasn't just locomotives and rolling stock that were preserved, but also some, at least, of the vast range of small structures, artefacts and documents that were an integral part of the total railway heritage. He was 'hands on' and combined his considerable skills with leadership and an organising ability that were inspirational.

Fred relaxes prior to the opening of MR 150 in the Midland Hotel in Derby in 1994.

There is scarcely any part of the Didcot Railway Centre we know today that has not felt the benefit of Fred's endeavours at some point over the years. He was also for many years the curator of Sir William McAlpine's private railway museum at Fawley. That was the day job (after his second retirement), while his 'hands on' work at Didcot continued. When it was suggested that I 'spoke to Fred' for advice about a preservation issue, he became involved with a third collection – this time a Midland one. It was Fred's experience, advice and practical help, so freely and enthusiastically given (on top of all his other activities), that guided the work of myself and my friends and colleagues in mounting the MR 150 exhibition in 1994 and all that followed. Eventually, only deteriorating health forced Fred to admit the existence in the English language of the word 'retirement'.

We spent many weekends at my house in 1993/94 planning, designing and selecting the objects and documents for MR 150. Saturday evening, after a full day's work, was the time to enjoy a meal and a scotch or three. On one such occasion I asked him what inspired his utter dedication to railway preservation over so many years. 'I did it for my mates; I came home, they didn't', was his reply. On their behalf, thank you, Fred.